# Worship
## *That Leads to the*
# Throne

## *Practical Strategies for Worship Leaders to Inspire Their Team & Usher People into God's Presence*

*Gerard Assey*

# Worship That Leads to the Throne:

***Practical Strategies for Worship Leaders to Inspire Their Team & Usher People into God's Presence***

By

Gerard Assey



*Published by:*
Gerard Assey
19/18, Palli Arasan Street
Anna Nagar East
Chennai - 600 102

**ISBN:** 978-81-986974-9-3

# Table of Contents

## Disclaimer:

*Any resemblance (names, characters, and scenarios used in this book, including testimonies and personal stories) to actual persons, living or dead, or actual events is purely coincidental. These examples are used solely for illustrative and teaching purposes.*

*The intent is to inspire and equip readers, not to depict real individuals or specific events. No harm or misrepresentation is intended.*

# Introduction

## Why This Book?

I still remember the moment I stepped onto the stage for the first time as a worship leader. The lights weren't dazzling, the microphone squealed just a little too much, and my knees felt like jelly. But the moment the first chord rang out and the congregation lifted their voices, I felt something shift—not just in the room, but inside me. I realized then that this wasn't just music. It wasn't just performance. It wasn't even about me leading people in songs. It was sacred. It was holy ground.

But somewhere along the way—between the hustle of Sunday morning rehearsals, the pressure to "bring the energy," and the constant pursuit of musical excellence—I began to lose sight of that holy moment. I began to wonder, how often do we as worship leaders truly pause to ask, "Is Jesus still at the center?"

That's what birthed this book.

## Restoring the Focus on God in Worship

We live in a time where the church is blessed with incredible musicians, gifted vocalists, and production capabilities that rival any concert stage. And yet, amid all this brilliance, we risk the greatest tragedy of all: a worship service where God is no longer the focus.

Worship is not about how good the harmonies sound or how smooth the transitions flow—though those things matter. Worship is about offering ourselves fully to God, tuning the heart before we tune the guitar. Worship is not a sound; it's a surrender.

In John 4:23-24, Jesus said,
*"Yet a time is coming and has now come when the true worshipers will worship the Father in the Spirit and in truth, for they are the kind of worshipers the Father seeks. God is spirit, and His worshipers must worship in the Spirit and in truth."*

The question is not, "How powerful was the setlist?" or "How many people sang along?" The real question is, "Was Jesus truly glorified?" If we walk away with goosebumps but no genuine encounter with God, we've missed the mark.

This book is written to help worship leaders realign everything—our planning, our teams, our hearts—with one focus: Jesus Christ.

**The Distractions of Modern Worship**

Let's be honest. Worship ministry today can be noisy—not just in sound, but in soul.

There's the pressure to "perform," to keep people engaged, to stay relevant. Social media highlights the best worship moments across the world, and it's easy to compare your small-town Sunday service with a viral Hillsong set on Instagram. There's the temptation to treat worship like a gig, the congregation like an audience, and the team like a band.

I've watched worship teams fall into performance traps. I've heard singers fret more about camera angles than consecration. I've seen leaders get more excited about a new loop pad than a new testimony. These are subtle shifts. But they can move us from being ministers to being entertainers.

The Old Testament gives us a clear warning in 2 Samuel 6, when Uzzah reached out to steady the Ark of the Covenant. Though his intentions may have seemed noble, his action disregarded the holiness of God's presence. And he paid the price. God's presence is not something we manage or manipulate—it's something we revere.

Worship is not about keeping up with the culture. It's about inviting people into the very presence of the King of Kings.

**Worship Leaders: Ministers to Both Team and Congregation**

One of the most misunderstood roles in the church today is that of the worship leader. You are not just a "music director" or someone who gets the service "hyped." You are a minister of the presence of God.

Your responsibility is twofold:

Minister to your team. These are the Levites entrusted to your care. Their growth, their spiritual well-being, and their understanding of worship often flow directly from your leadership. It is your job to disciple them, not just direct them musically.

Minister to the congregation. You are leading people somewhere—either closer to God, or away from Him. Each song choice, each spoken word, each posture matters. You are the shepherd of the worship moment, guiding people into an encounter with the Living God.

Consider the example of King David, who was both a skilled musician and a man after God's own heart. When he brought the Ark back to Jerusalem in 2 Samuel 6, he danced with all his might before the Lord. He wasn't performing; he was leading in worship by example. His passion was contagious, his heart sincere. That's what the people followed.

In the New Testament, Paul and Silas worshipped in a prison cell (Acts 16:25). Their worship didn't rely on lighting or instruments—it was raw, real, and powerful. And God responded. Chains broke. Doors opened. Souls were saved. That's the kind of worship leadership this world is starving for.

**My Journey in Worship Leadership**

If I'm honest, I didn't start out with all the right motives. I loved music. I loved the atmosphere of church. I loved the attention that came with standing on stage. But it wasn't until I hit a wall in ministry—a season where my songs felt empty and my soul felt dry—that I truly encountered what worship really was.

I remember one particular Sunday. We had just finished a technically flawless set. Every note was in place, the team sounded amazing, and the crowd responded. But as I walked off the platform, I felt... nothing. It was like I had just performed, but God hadn't shown up. That night, I fell to my knees and prayed, "God, if You're not in this, I don't want it anymore."

That was the beginning of a slow, painful, beautiful transformation. I stopped trying to impress people and started trying to please God. I began to disciple my team. I started leading worship off stage before I did it on stage. And I saw the Spirit move in ways I never imagined.

One of my team members, a young guitarist, came to me months later with tears in his eyes and said, *"For the first time, I feel like I actually worship God through my playing. It's not about the beat or strum anymore—it's about His presence."*

That's when I knew. This is what I was born to do—to help others discover what true, Spirit-filled worship looks like.

**Why This Book Matters Right Now**

In a world where attention spans are short, distractions are everywhere, and "church" is often packaged for consumption, we need worship leaders who will call the church back to the heart of worship.

This book is not a "how to impress your congregation" manual. It's not a checklist for flawless transitions or fancy gear. This is a guide to shepherding hearts—your team's and your church's—back to Jesus.

It's filled with stories, Scripture, examples, and practical strategies. But more than that, it's a call. A sacred summons. To lead differently. To lead deeply. To lead with the presence of God as your highest goal.

Because when we center our worship on Jesus, we don't just sing songs.

We encounter Heaven.

# Part I:
# Motivating and Engaging the Worship Team

# Chapter 1: Cultivating a Christ-Centered Team Culture

The first time I met my new worship team at Throne Room Worship, I felt like I'd walked into a band rehearsal more than a ministry gathering. There was laughter, inside jokes, and incredible musical talent—but spiritually, the room felt empty. Something was missing. We had the sound of worship but not the spirit of it.

It didn't take long to realize what was off. The team had culture, yes—but it wasn't Christ-centered. They were talented, passionate about music, and committed to excellence, but the culture wasn't one of ministry. It was a culture of performance. And that's a dangerous place for any worship team to live in.

Culture is what happens when no one is watching—the unseen glue that holds a team together or silently pushes it apart. As a worship leader, your job is not just to direct sound. You're called to cultivate the culture of your team. That culture must be rooted in Christ, not charisma.

**Why Culture Matters More Than Talent**

Let me be blunt: I'd rather lead worship with five humble, God-fearing amateurs than with five Grammy-level musicians who carry pride and division. Skill can be taught. Heart cannot.

In 1 Samuel 16, when the prophet Samuel was sent to anoint the next king of Israel, he was impressed by the appearance of Eliab. But God said:

*"Do not consider his appearance or his height, for I have rejected him. The Lord does not look at the things people look at. People look at the outward appearance, but the Lord looks at the heart."* (1 Samuel 16:7)

That same principle applies to your team. God is more interested in our posture than our performance. A team can sound heavenly and still be spiritually hollow. But a team with hearts aligned to Christ—even if their skill is still developing—will carry a presence that no rehearsal can produce.

I once knew a background vocalist named Lydia. She didn't have the strongest voice on the team, but every time she sang, something in the room shifted. Not because she hit every note perfectly, but because she worshipped from the depths of her soul. Her posture in private overflowed in public.

Talent impresses people. Character invites the presence of God.

**Establishing a Purpose Bigger Than Music**

One of the first things I did with my new team was gather them—not for rehearsal, but for prayer. I asked a simple question:

*"Why do you do this?"*

The answers varied:

*"I love to sing."*

*"I've always been part of a band."*

*"I feel like this is how I serve."*

All valid. But none of them pointed to our true purpose: to glorify Jesus and lead others into His presence.

A Christ-centered worship team understands that we're not here to "do church" or "play good music." We are here to build altars, like Abraham, Isaac, and

Jacob did—places of sacrifice where people can encounter the living God.

In the Old Testament, the tribe of Levi was set apart not for their musical ability, but for their dedication to serve in God's presence (Numbers 3:5–10). Their role was sacred. It wasn't about songs; it was about sanctity. That same call rests on us today.

As a team, we began reshaping our language. Rehearsals became "preparation for the presence." Sound checks were seen as stewardship of what God had given us. Sunday wasn't "performance day"—it was mission day.

Our purpose became bigger than music. We weren't performers. We were priests.

**Core Values: Humility, Unity, and Reverence**

If you want to cultivate a Christ-centered culture, you must build it on kingdom values. In our team, we identified three foundational values—humility, unity, and reverence.

Humility is not thinking less of ourselves; it's thinking of ourselves less. It's being teachable, open to correction, and more concerned about glorifying God than shining on stage. In Philippians 2:3, Paul urges, *"Do nothing out of selfish ambition or vain conceit. Rather, in humility value others above yourselves."*

I remember in one of the churches, one Sunday, the lead guitarist, Nathan—a gifted, Berklee-trained musician—offered to step down for a newer, less experienced guitarist named Aaron. Why? I was told later that it was because he sensed Aaron needed the encouragement and opportunity. That act of humility spoke louder than any solo ever could.

Unity means we are one body, with one heart. When there's disunity on the team—hidden offense,

comparison, competition—it shows up in worship. Psalm 133 says,
*"How good and pleasant it is when God's people live together in unity... For there the Lord bestows His blessing."*
We made a commitment: We resolve conflict before we rehearse. No rehearsing while hearts are bitter. No pretending things are fine when they're not. Our unity became sacred. And as we honored that, we saw God bless our worship in ways we never expected.
Reverence is about remembering who this is all for. Not the pastor. Not the congregation. Not the livestream audience. It's for Jesus. Always Jesus.
In Acts 5, Ananias and Sapphira pretended to give everything to God, but held back in secret. The result was tragic. God is not interested in partial worship. He wants our whole hearts. Reverence reminds us that we're not just doing something artistic—we're standing before a holy God.

**Creating Shared Spiritual Goals (Not Just Musical Ones)**

One of the turning points in our team culture came when we began setting spiritual goals together—not just musical ones. It started with a simple conversation:
"What do we want our worship to accomplish in the lives of people?"
The answers were profound:
*"We want people to encounter healing."*
*"We want to see people set free from shame."*
*"We want Jesus to be glorified, not us."*
So, we created a rhythm: once a month, we gathered not to rehearse—but to reflect, pray, and dream

spiritually. We shared testimonies of what God was doing. We prayed for the congregation by name. We fasted before special services. We celebrated not when a song went smoothly, but when someone gave their life to Christ during worship.

In that season, I watched my team transform. Not just musically. Spiritually.

We weren't just a team anymore. We were a family. We cried together. We carried one another's burdens. We rejoiced when someone shared a breakthrough. Our Sunday sets became overflow from our Monday through Saturday walk with Jesus.

**What Kind of Culture Are You Cultivating?**

Culture isn't built overnight. It's not shaped by one sermon or set. It's shaped by a thousand small decisions—a quiet prayer before rehearsal, a gentle correction in love, a team member stepping down for the good of another, a shared moment of worship in someone's living room.

Ask yourself:

*What's the dominant spirit of your team?*

*Is it competition or camaraderie?*

*Insecurity or identity?*

*Performance or presence?*

As a worship leader, you have the sacred responsibility to build what God can bless. Not a perfect team. But a Christ-centered one.

You won't always get it right. I certainly haven't. But every time we take a step toward Christ in our team culture, we take a step closer to worship that moves heaven and transforms earth.

Let this be the cry of your heart as a worship leader:

*“Lord, build in us what will glorify You. Shape in us a team that reflects You. Let our sound rise from hearts that burn for You.”*

# Chapter 2: Spiritual Formation of the Worship Team

When people look at a worship team on stage, they see the polished final product—blended harmonies, smooth transitions, powerful vocal moments, and skilled musicianship. What they don't see is what happens off stage, behind the scenes, in the quiet spaces where souls are being formed and leaders are being refined.

Spiritual formation is the soul of your sound. Without it, worship becomes noise. With it, worship becomes an offering.

One of the Worship leaders, I know personally, shared how he learned this truth the hard way. He mentioned of how early in ministry, he focused so much on rehearsals, arrangements, and Sunday service flow that he neglected the inner life of his team. He went on to say that they were musically tight but spiritually dry. These were his words of caution:*"It wasn't until we faced a crisis—a worship leader named Sam walked away from the faith after leading worship for years—that I was forced to ask: What are we really building here?*

He continued: "*That was the moment everything shifted for me. I realized that as a worship leader, I am not just a musical director. I am a spiritual shepherd. And shepherds don't just lead songs. They lead souls"*

## The Foundation: Daily and Weekly Spiritual Disciplines

The spiritual formation of a worship team doesn't begin at rehearsal. It begins in the personal devotion of each member.

Let's talk honestly. Life is busy. Our team members juggle full-time jobs, families, studies, and other responsibilities. But a team that doesn't have time for Jesus Monday through Saturday can't expect to lead others into His presence on Sunday.

I often tell my team: "We minister from the overflow, not the deficit."

In Daniel 6:10, when King Darius signed a decree forbidding prayer to any god except himself, Daniel didn't panic or argue. He simply went to his room, opened his window toward Jerusalem, and continued to pray three times a day—*just as he had done before*. Daniel's consistency in spiritual discipline gave him the strength to stand in the lion's den without fear.

Worship leaders and team members need that same depth of consistency—daily prayer, scripture reading, listening to God's voice, and times of stillness. These disciplines are not religious checkboxes; they are lifelines to intimacy with God.

In our team, we began something called *"The First Fifteen"*—a challenge where every team member committed to giving the first 15 minutes of their day to God. No phones, no social media, no work—just God. Those small, daily deposits began to produce a huge spiritual return.

## Praying Together as a Team

One of the most powerful shifts in our team happened when we made prayer a non-negotiable part of every gathering.

Before rehearsals, before soundchecks, before even discussing the setlist, we gather in a circle, hold hands or place a hand on each other's shoulders, and pray. Sometimes the prayers are short and practical—"God, help us to focus and serve well tonight." Other times, someone begins to weep, a word is shared, and we find ourselves on our knees, undone in the presence of God.

This was what happened one Thursday evening when Mariah, a backup vocalist, burst into tears during prayer. She had been struggling with anxiety and hadn't told anyone. But in that moment of collective prayer, she felt safe enough to share. The team rallied around her, laid hands on her, and prayed with passion. That moment knit our hearts together in a way no musical moment ever could.

In Acts 4:31, after the early believers prayed, the place where they were meeting shook, and they were all filled with the Holy Spirit and spoke the word of God boldly. That's the power of unified prayer. It shakes the ground beneath us. It releases boldness. It transforms the atmosphere.

When worship teams pray together, they don't just prepare songs—they prepare sanctuaries.

## Scripture Meditation for Worship Leaders

A worship leader without the Word is like a singer with no breath. The very songs we sing are often rooted in Scripture—so how can we lead people into God's truth if we're not immersed in it ourselves?

When Jesus was tempted in the wilderness (Matthew 4), He didn't respond with emotion or opinion. He responded with Scripture: "It is written..." He knew the Word. He lived it. He breathed it.

I once encouraged my team to choose a psalm each week and meditate on it. Not just read it—meditate. One week, we chose Psalm 63. I asked everyone to sit with the passage every day for a week. No deep study. No commentary. Just read, reflect, listen, and respond.

The following Sunday, we sang *"Draw Me Close to You."* But something was different. The words weren't just lyrics anymore—they were prayers, anchored in Scripture. Several people in the congregation wept during that worship set. One later told me, "It felt like you were singing the cry of my heart."

That's the power of Scripture meditation. It shapes the inner life of the worshiper. It turns songs into sacred moments.

Give your team small, bite-sized Scriptures to reflect on weekly. Encourage journaling, or voice-note reflections. It's not about being theological experts. It's about being spiritually awake.

**Team Devotions and Accountability**

One of the most transformative practices in our team has been weekly devotions and monthly check-ins.

Every week, one team member rotates and shares a short devotion—just 5–7 minutes—on what God has been teaching them. Sometimes it's a Scripture, other times a personal testimony, or a lesson from a failure. What matters is that we're feeding one another spiritually.

One Sunday, Marcus, a quiet keyboardist, shared about his struggle with pride. He talked about how he felt jealous when someone else led a song he thought he deserved. He confessed it before us with humility and tears. We prayed over him, encouraged him, and that day—he played with more freedom and joy than we had ever seen.

This is the essence of accountability: honest confession, mutual encouragement, and spiritual covering.

James 5:16 says,

*"Confess your sins to each other and pray for each other so that you may be healed. The prayer of a righteous person is powerful and effective."*

Accountability isn't about catching people in sin. It's about protecting their purpose. It's about helping each other finish well.

To foster this, we created "anchor partners"—one-on-one prayer and encouragement pairs who would check in weekly. These weren't therapy sessions, just sacred friendships. They'd ask, "How's your walk with Jesus?" "What are you struggling with?" "How can I pray for you today?"

These relationships didn't just strengthen individuals—they fortified the entire team.

**A Spirit-Formed Team Carries Revival**

Spiritual formation isn't glamorous. It's slow. It's hidden. It often feels like digging a well in dry ground. But when the rains come—and they will—it becomes a reservoir of living water, not just for your team, but for your entire church.

A musically excellent team can impress people. But a spiritually formed team can shift the heavens.

In John 4, Jesus told the woman at the well that the Father seeks those who will worship Him in spirit and in truth. That's what this chapter is about. That's what your calling is about.

Not just getting the music right. But getting the heart right.

So build your team not just with rehearsals and setlists, but with prayer and Scripture. With honesty and accountability. With devotion and consistency.

*Because when the lights dim, the stage fades, and the music stops—it's the heart that remains.*

# Chapter 3:
# The Role of Relationship and Community

If you've ever been part of a worship team, you know this truth all too well: music may be what brings people together, but it's not what keeps them together. That glue—that sacred, mysterious, divine glue—is relationship.

Before the first chord is strummed, before the setlist is discussed, before the lights and lyrics are cued, there is something far more foundational—a sense of belonging. A worship team isn't just a collection of gifted individuals. It is a community of worshipers. And that makes all the difference.

I remember a particular season in our worship ministry when everything looked perfect on the outside. Our harmonies were on point, our transitions seamless, and the congregation seemed fully engaged. But something felt... hollow. As the team leader, I couldn't quite put my finger on it—until I realized that while we had built a musically excellent team, we had neglected to build a spiritually connected family.

We were performers together, not pilgrims together.

That's when I knew something had to change.

## The Power of Belonging: Building Friendships, Not Just Partnerships

In Genesis 2:18, God said, "It is not good for man to be alone." And He wasn't just talking about marriage—He was identifying the deep human need for connection. Even in the Garden, even in perfection, community was essential.

A worship team that lacks relational depth will always feel like a job. But a team that becomes a spiritual family? That's where joy, unity, and God's presence flourish.

Let me tell you about Daniel and Kris. They were both vocalists on a team I knew of—talented, passionate, but wildly different. Daniel was introverted and reflective, while Kris was energetic and loud. At first, they avoided each other like oil and water. But one night after rehearsal, they were invited to grab dinner. They ended up sitting across from each other, reluctantly making small talk. That conversation turned into shared laughter over tacos, and weeks later, a strong friendship had blossomed.

Months down the line, we were told of how they were leading a song together in perfect harmony—not just musically, but in spirit. Something had changed. It wasn't just rehearsed unity; it was relational unity. That's the fruit of friendship.

In Acts 2:42–47, the early church wasn't just known for their doctrine or miracles, but for their fellowship—breaking bread in each other's homes, praying, and sharing life. And the result? "The Lord added to their number daily those who were being saved."

God breathes on unity, and unity grows from relationship.

**How Love and Trust Increase Participation and Ownership**

People don't commit deeply to what they don't feel emotionally connected to. That's true in every area of life—including worship ministry.

When a team member feels seen, loved, and heard, their level of participation moves from compliance to ownership. They're no longer just showing up for a scheduled slot. They're showing up for each other—and ultimately, for Jesus.

One Sunday, a drummer Elijah showed up late and flustered. He had just found out his grandmother was diagnosed with cancer. The easy response would've been to keep things "professional" and move on with the service. But instead, the team stopped everything- gathered around him, prayed for his family, and asked what he needed. He played that morning with tears in his eyes, but his heart was held together by the love of a team that cared.

When Jesus washed His disciples' foot in John 13, He wasn't just teaching humility—He was building a new kind of culture. One where leadership flowed from love, and greatness was expressed through service. He told them, "By this everyone will know that you are my disciples, if you love one another" (John 13:35).

That kind of love doesn't just grow on stage. It grows over time, trust, and shared experiences.

I once asked my team during a retreat: "If worship disappeared tomorrow—no music, no microphones, no services—would we still have a reason to gather?" That question stopped everyone in their tracks. It forced us to reflect: *Are we here for the music or the mission? Are we just teammates, or are we a family?*

**Practical Ideas for Strengthening Community**

Let me offer a few things we started doing that transformed our team from simply functional to deeply relational. You don't need a big budget. You just need intentionality.

**1. Team Retreats:**

Once a year, we take a weekend away—phones off, agendas set aside—and focus on worship, testimony, and fun. It's not about perfection; it's about presence. One year, we stayed in a small retreat center, and each person shared their story—how they met Jesus, their struggles, and why they worship. Walls came down. Tears flowed. Hearts were knit together.

Retreats remind us that behind every microphone is a miracle—a life that's been touched by grace.

**2. Shared Meals:**

Never underestimate the power of food! Whether it's post-rehearsal pizza or a Sunday brunch, meals provide space for organic conversations and deepening connections. Jesus often ministered around meals—whether feeding the 5,000 or eating with sinners. Meals create margin. They slow us down enough to truly see each other.

**3. Serving Together Beyond the Stage:**

We began volunteering as a team—helping with outreach programs, serving at a homeless shelter, or supporting another ministry in the church. One time, we helped clean up a flooded community center. There, in muddy jeans and soaked shoes, we discovered a deeper bond. Serving together off the platform made our worship on the platform more sincere.

**4. Celebrate Milestones and Support One Another:**

Birthdays, engagements, tough seasons, and victories—celebrate them. One of our vocalists, Leah, was the first in her family to graduate college.

We surprised her with a small party after rehearsal. That moment said, "You matter beyond your voice. You matter because you're ours."

This isn't just nice Christian kindness—it's kingdom culture. It's the embodiment of Romans 12:15: "Rejoice with those who rejoice; mourn with those who mourn."

**More Than a Team—A Spiritual Family**

Worship is not a performance. It's a spiritual offering. And behind that offering must be a people who are anchored in love, bound in community, and committed to each other's growth.

Relationships take work. There will be misunderstandings, offenses, and personality clashes. But when we choose grace over gossip, unity over ego, and love over isolation, something beautiful happens: God commands His blessing (Psalm 133).

So let me ask you, as a worship leader or team member:

- ✓ *Do your teammates know you as a person, not just a player?*
- ✓ *Are you creating spaces for trust to be built?*
- ✓ *Are you modeling a kind of community that reflects the heart of Jesus?*

*Because when a team becomes a family, and that family lifts up Jesus together—heaven touches earth.*

# Chapter 4:
# Preparing the Heart Before the Stage

Worship doesn't begin when the lights dim or the first chord rings out from a guitar. It doesn't even begin at rehearsal or when the team enters the sanctuary. True worship begins in the heart—in the quiet, often unseen places where our motives, affections, and attitudes are formed.

Too often, the modern church culture can unintentionally foster a performance mindset in worship leaders and teams. We fine-tune our harmonies, align our clicks and cues, and polish every moment of a set—yet, if the heart isn't prepared, we risk offering something that is technically excellent but spiritually empty. What good is a perfectly executed set if it flows from a distracted or divided heart?

This chapter isn't about rehearsals or song lists. It's about the sacred inner work of preparing the heart before we ever step on stage. Because in the kingdom of God, the platform is not a stage for display—it is an altar of surrender.

**Weekly Team Preparation Rituals (Spiritual and Technical)**

I'll never forget the week I learned the importance of *preparation with presence*. Our team had been struggling—technically, we were fine, but something felt off. I called for a team meeting before rehearsal. No instruments, no in-ears. Just us, a circle of chairs, and an open Bible.

We read Psalm 24 together—"Who may ascend the hill of the Lord? Who may stand in His holy place?

He who has clean hands and a pure heart..." Then we just sat. No agenda. Just silence and waiting on God. Some began to cry. Others confessed feeling spiritually dry. It was raw, but it was real. That night, we didn't just rehearse—we ministered to each other and to God. The next Sunday, the atmosphere shifted. Not because of new songs, but because we came with hearts already bowed.

Since then, we adopted a simple rhythm: 30 minutes of soul work before technical work. We begin our weekly rehearsals with Scripture, prayer, and personal check-ins. It might be one person sharing a verse that's stirring them or a prayer of thanksgiving for what God did that week. It sets the tone. It reminds us: *We're not just singers or musicians. We're priests bringing an offering.*

The Old Testament priests never approached the tabernacle casually. In Exodus 30, God instructed that Aaron and his sons were to wash before entering the tent of meeting so that they would not die. It was a physical act pointing to a spiritual reality: purity and preparation matter when you step into sacred spaces.

We're not under the Old Covenant anymore—but the principle still echoes. We must never treat the sacred as common.

**Heart Checks and Spiritual Readiness**

Preparation begins with a question we should all ask ourselves: "Why am I doing this?"

Is it to sound great? Be seen? Or is it truly to lift high the name of Jesus?

Sometimes I've had to ask hard questions of myself and my team. I remember asking Jordan, our electric guitarist, "How's your heart, really?" He paused.

Tears welled up. "Honestly, I'm struggling. I've been coming here, playing, but I haven't opened my Bible in weeks. I feel like a fraud."

We didn't scold him. We prayed. We reminded him that he was more than his gift—he was a son of God. That conversation didn't just heal something in Jordan. It reshaped our entire team culture. We realized the greatest preparation is inner alignment—not just musical excellence.

Jesus warned in Matthew 15:8, "These people honor me with their lips, but their hearts are far from me." That verse is sobering for any worship leader. It reminds us that God doesn't just hear our voices—He searches our motives.

This is why regular "heart checks" are vital. It could be as simple as taking a few minutes before rehearsal to ask:

- ✓ *"Is there any pride or comparison in me?"*
- ✓ *"Am I carrying offense toward someone on this team?"*
- ✓ *"Have I spent time with God outside of this room?"*

Spiritual readiness isn't about perfection. It's about posture—a heart bowed low before a holy God.

### The Role of Confession and Purity in Effective Worship Leadership

Confession is not a popular topic in modern worship circles, but it is essential. Not as a performance of piety, but as a pathway to freedom.

In Psalm 51, after David's moral failure, he cried out to God: "Create in me a clean heart, O God, and renew a steadfast spirit within me… Then I will teach transgressors Your ways, and sinners will be converted to You." (Psalm 51:10-13)

Notice the order. Cleansing comes before ministry. Purity precedes power. David understood that effective ministry flows from a heart made clean.

There was a time in our worship ministry when two team members—Ava and Noah—were in conflict. They had a disagreement over a scheduling issue that had gone unresolved. Week after week, they led worship together, but the tension was felt. Eventually, I pulled them aside and gently challenged them to talk. What started as a tense meeting ended in repentance and reconciliation. Ava wept and said, "I've been asking God why I feel so distant during worship. I didn't realize my unforgiveness was in the way."

After that, our worship felt different—lighter, freer, more genuine. That's the power of confession.

James 5:16 reminds us, "*Confess your sins to one another and pray for one another, that you may be healed.*" The effectiveness of our worship is tied to the health of our hearts and relationships.

Purity isn't about rule-following—it's about intimacy. It clears the fog between us and the face of God.

**Preparing the Inner Altar**

As worship leaders, we are not merely preparing for a performance—we are preparing to stand in the gap, to usher in the presence of the King, to model surrender before a watching church. But we cannot take others where we ourselves have not gone.

The Israelites offered daily sacrifices on the altar, but now, under the New Covenant, we are the living sacrifice (Romans 12:1). And that means preparing ourselves—body, soul, and spirit—to offer something holy, not hollow.

Before the platform, before the lights, before the first note is played—let the heart be the first altar we prepare.

*Because if our hearts are clean, our worship will carry weight.*

*And that's the kind of worship that not only fills a room with sound—it shifts atmospheres, breaks chains, and brings glory to the only One worthy of it all.*

# Chapter 5: Equipping and Empowering Team Members

One of the greatest privileges of being a worship leader is not just leading songs, but raising leaders. The modern Church is filled with gifted musicians, talented singers, and capable technicians—but what the Lord desires are *true worshippers* (John 4:23), those who lead not from the platform first, but from the secret place.

In many worship ministries, it's easy to settle for excellence in music while overlooking excellence in spiritual depth and character. But the heart of true worship is discipleship—equipping people to know God deeply and lead others from that place.

Let me tell you a story about one of my friends former team members, Joshua. He came to their worship team audition with raw passion and musical fire. His voice was powerful, and he could command a room effortlessly. But within weeks, it became clear that while he was musically prepared, he was spiritually underdeveloped. He saw worship leading more like a performance than a priestly assignment. He would show up late to rehearsals, bristle at constructive feedback, and once even said to another team member, "I don't need to prepare spiritually. I bring the energy. That's enough."

My friend had a choice to make—either let him continue, for the sake of his voice and stage presence, or pause and disciple him. He chose the latter. For the next few months, Joshua didn't sing on Sundays. Instead, he sat in on team devotions, read through the Psalms with my friend, and volunteered behind the scenes. At first, he resisted. But over time, we saw his heart begin to break in the right places. He started asking deeper questions. He began to pray aloud with more humility than flair. And eventually, he led again—this time, not as a star, but as a servant. The congregation noticed. *God's presence was different on him.*

That's what equipping truly looks like. It's not just about giving people a microphone. It's about training hearts to carry the weight of glory.

**Training the Team Beyond Music: Theology of Worship**

If we want to build a team that doesn't just perform songs but understands worship, we have to go beyond technique and talk about theology—the study of who God is and what He desires.

In the Old Testament, we see that worship was never man-centered. From Moses to David, from the Tabernacle to the Temple, the focus was always on God's holiness and the need for reverent offering. In Leviticus 10, when Nadab and Abihu brought "unauthorized fire" before the Lord, they were struck down—not because they sang off-key or missed a chord, but because they didn't approach God with proper understanding and reverence.

Many on our worship teams may not know why we raise our hands, kneel, or repeat certain phrases. They may not understand that worship is a response to revelation—that we sing *because* God is good, *because* He's faithful, *because* He sent His Son.

I started incorporating short teachings during rehearsal nights—nothing fancy, just 10-minute devotionals on themes like the fear of the Lord, the role of the Levites, or why Jesus cleansed the Temple. One night, we read Revelation 4–5 together. As we pictured the throne, the living creatures crying "Holy," and the elders casting crowns, one of our newer singers, Hannah, whispered, "I've never realized how holy God is... I don't think I've ever led worship with that in mind."

That moment changed her forever. Now she prepares not just musically, but theologically—with reverence, awe, and a heart that wants to honor the One seated on the throne.

**Giving Opportunities for Growth and Leadership**

Empowering a team means giving people room to grow, fail, and try again.

When I first started, I used to think I had to do everything—the planning, the leading, the praying, the transitions. But over time, I realized that when I hold too tightly to every aspect of leadership, I become a bottleneck for others' growth.

I remember giving Jenna—one of our background vocalists—a chance to lead a song one Sunday. She was nervous. "What if I mess up the timing?" she asked. "What if I forget the lyrics?" I told her, "That's okay. Worship isn't about flawless delivery. It's about faithful offering."

That Sunday, she led with trembling hands—but with a soft, surrendered heart. And the congregation responded—not because the note was perfect, but because the spirit was genuine. She walked off the platform in tears. "I felt God so close," she said.

Giving people opportunity builds *ownership*, and ownership builds *maturity*.

Even Jesus did this. He didn't do all the ministry Himself. He sent out the seventy-two (Luke 10) and entrusted them with authority. Did they get it all right? No. But they came back filled with joy and humility, having learned the power of obedience.

We must create safe spaces for people to step out. It's not about their perfection—it's about their posture.

**Dealing with Ego, Performance Mentality, and Insecurity**

Every worship team deals with three silent saboteurs: ego, performance, and insecurity.

Ego says, *"I need to be seen."*

Performance says, *"I need to impress."*

Insecurity says, *"I'm not good enough unless I perform well."*

Each one is a distortion of identity.

My friend once had a drummer named Marcus who struggled with performance anxiety. Every Sunday, he would obsess over getting the tempo just right. If he missed a beat, his whole mood would spiral. My friend pulled him aside one week and asked, "Marcus, why do you feel so shaken when you mess up?" He said, "Because I feel like I let God down. And I feel like people won't respect me."

That was an open door. My friend reminded him that God's love is not earned by flawless drumming, and that worship isn't a concert—it's a conversation with heaven. They prayed together, and spoke identity over him: "You're not a drummer first. You're a son. You worship through drumming, but your worth isn't in what you play."

Similarly, I've had to confront ego—gently, but firmly. When someone is making worship about themselves, you can feel it. It's no longer an offering—it's a performance.

The cure for both ego and insecurity is the same: intimacy with Jesus. When we know who He is and who we are in Him, we don't need the spotlight—and we're not crushed when we don't get it.

**Encouraging Each Team Member to Be a Worshipper First**

At the end of the day, this is the goal: to create a team full of worshippers, not just worship leaders.

I tell my team often, "If you don't love worship when no one's watching, you have no business leading when everyone's looking." True worshippers don't need a platform to pour out praise. They do it in their rooms, in their cars, in the kitchen.

Jesus told the woman at the well that the Father is looking for worshippers, not performers (John 4:23). Not even worship leaders—just *worshippers*. That means anyone on your team—from the sound tech to the vocalist—is called to the same standard: worship first, leadership second.

We once had a team night where I asked everyone to come with no instruments, no planning. Just bring your Bibles and hearts. We lit some candles, turned off the lights, and spent the evening singing spontaneous songs, reading Scripture, and sharing testimonies. There was no plan. No song list. Just presence.

And something sacred happened: we became a room of worshippers again.

**Raising Worshippers, Not Performers**

Equipping and empowering your team is not a one-time event. It's a culture, a commitment, and a calling. It's saying, "We are not here to perform. We are here to host the presence of the Living God."

When your team knows this—when they believe it deep down—everything changes. The atmosphere shifts. The room fills with awe. And Jesus takes center stage, just as He deserves.

And as a leader, that is your greatest joy: to watch your team rise—not for their glory, but for His.

Because when the Church is led by true worshippers, the world will encounter the glory of God.

# Chapter 6: Encouraging Ownership and Initiative

Some of the most powerful worship moments don't happen because of one person's vision—they happen when a team of worshippers steps in, each bringing their hearts, ideas, and gifts to the table. The Spirit of God loves to move where there is unity, humility, and shared responsibility.

Leadership is never meant to be a solo act. Worship leadership—especially—is a sacred collaboration between individuals who are each carrying their portion of the flame. And when every team member feels seen, heard, and trusted to contribute, something extraordinary happens: the weight of ministry is shared, and the joy of ministry multiplies.

I remember early in my ministry days, I (like many worship leaders) felt the pressure to do it all—choose the set list, organize the rehearsal, lead every song, manage the transitions, coordinate the tech, and make sure the lights weren't too blinding. It was exhausting. But even worse, it was robbing others of the joy of participation. I had unknowingly created a dependent culture, not a collaborative one.

That's when I began to shift. I started inviting others into the process, asking questions like: *"What do you feel the Lord is saying for this week?"* or *"Would you like to lead one of the songs?"* Slowly but surely, team members started to rise. What I thought would result in chaos actually birthed creativity, depth, and stronger spiritual ownership.

**How to Lead Collaboratively: A Biblical Model**

In Exodus 17, Moses is holding up his hands while Joshua fights in the valley. As long as Moses' hands were raised, Israel prevailed. But when he grew weary, the tide turned. What changed the battle was not Moses pulling more strength from within—it was Aaron and Hur coming alongside him and holding up his arms.

That's a picture of collaborative leadership. It's not about one person carrying everything—it's about shared strength.

In the New Testament, Paul rarely traveled or ministered alone. He had Timothy, Silas, Barnabas, Luke, and others. Even Jesus modeled this when He sent His disciples out two by two. Why? Because the Kingdom was always meant to be built in partnership. When worship leadership becomes collaborative, the burden is lifted, and the ministry becomes more sustainable. More than that, it becomes joyful.

Let me introduce you to a worship team I served alongside in a city called Calvary Heights. The team was led by a couple named Arvind and Sharon. They had intentionally cultivated a culture where the entire team—from vocalists to techs—participated in planning and prayer. Every Tuesday night, they had "Worship Roundtable"—a time not just to rehearse, but to dream together, read Scripture, and ask, *"What is the Lord highlighting this week?"*

One week, their bass player—yes, the quiet guy in the corner—felt impressed to share Psalm 40:3: "He put a new song in my mouth, a hymn of praise to our God." It resonated with the room, and from that verse came a new spontaneous chorus that became their anthem for weeks. If leadership had remained top-down, that song might never have surfaced. But because space was created, heaven touched earth through the voice of someone who rarely spoke.

**Creating Space for Team Input and Creativity**

Creativity thrives in environments where people feel safe, valued, and invited.

The challenge many leaders face is the fear of losing control. What if someone suggests something strange? What if they choose a song I wouldn't pick? What if it doesn't sound polished?

But the truth is—creativity is often messy before it's beautiful.

I recall a worship leader named Eliana who led a youth band. Her team was talented, but disengaged. She realized that though she was managing everything efficiently, she had left no room for their ideas. So she began something she called "Vision Night." Once a month, the team would bring a song, a Scripture, or a visual they felt inspired by. Sometimes it was chaotic. Sometimes no one brought anything. But slowly, they warmed up. Her keyboardist began composing original intros. A shy vocalist began writing devotional thoughts to read before songs. Her team became alive—not just performers, but partners in the vision.

God is a Creator. If we are made in His image, we too are called to create. When your team feels empowered to dream with you, they begin to carry the vision—not just follow it.

**Rotations and Shared Responsibility**

Burnout is real. But so is boredom.

If the same person leads worship every week, it's easy to fall into routine—or even entitlement. Shared responsibility solves both problems.

By implementing rotations, team members have time to prepare deeply, rest well, and bring fresh energy when it's their turn. It also encourages development. New leaders rise when given the chance to serve in smaller capacities first.

I once worked with a church that had four worship teams rotating weekly. The newer musicians were paired with seasoned ones, and every person had a turn to lead prayer, share a verse, or speak during transitions. It wasn't always perfect—but it was powerful. People grew. And there was no celebrity culture—just a family of worshippers.

Shared responsibility also means involving the team in non-musical roles. Who's helping with planning? Who's mentoring the younger ones? Who's organizing the devotional calendar? When people have ownership over different aspects, they invest with more heart.

**Monthly Evaluations and Open Feedback Loops**

Feedback is not criticism—it's a gift. But only in the right culture.

In many teams, evaluation feels like a dreaded performance review. But when done well, it can be a life-giving practice of mutual growth.

David, in Psalm 139, prayed, "Search me, O God, and know my heart... see if there is any offensive way in me." Feedback is that kind of search—not to shame, but to refine.

I once implemented monthly check-ins with my worship team. We sat with tea, talked about the month, and reflected on three things:

- ✓ What went well?
- ✓ What could be better?
- ✓ How can we support each other?

To make it safe, I always went first—sharing my own mistakes or missteps from the platform. Vulnerability created space for honesty without fear. Team members began opening up: “I was rushing transitions.” “I haven’t been preparing spiritually.” “I need help managing my nerves.”

Because it was consistent, it became normal. No one felt attacked. Instead, they felt loved enough to be challenged.

In fact, it was during one of these check-ins that a young vocalist said, “I think I’m supposed to start mentoring the newer singers.” I hadn’t thought of him in that way before—but he saw something in himself. That’s ownership in action.

**From Volunteers to Vision Carriers**

There’s a big difference between someone who shows up for a slot and someone who shows up for a mission.

Our job as leaders is not to just assign tasks, but to awaken hearts. When we empower our teams to lead with us, dream with us, create with us, and reflect with us—we’re not just building a good worship team. We’re building a kingdom-minded family of worshippers who know they belong.

And when that happens? The worship goes deeper. The songs carry more weight. And the glory doesn’t fall on one person—it rests on the whole house.

Because when every hand is on deck, and every heart is engaged, God dwells there.

# Chapter 7: Encouraging Excellence Without Idolizing Perfection

Worship is holy. It is a sacred moment where human hearts reach toward a holy God, and heaven touches earth. Naturally, as worship leaders, we desire to offer God our very best. We want the harmonies to be tight, the transitions smooth, the sound system flawless, and the team well-prepared. And rightly so.

But somewhere along the way, if we are not careful, the pursuit of excellence can morph into an obsession with perfection—and when that happens, worship becomes a performance, not a sacrifice. The presence of God gets drowned out by the pressure to get everything "just right." Instead of leading people to the throne, we end up leading them to our well-polished presentation.

This chapter is a gentle but necessary call to hold excellence in one hand and grace in the other, remembering that God does not require our perfection—He desires our surrender.

## God Delights in Excellence, Not Perfectionism

Let's begin with a truth that sets us free: God never called us to be perfect performers; He called us to be faithful worshippers.

In the Old Testament, we see God commanding His people to bring offerings without blemish (Leviticus 22:21). This wasn't because God expected flawless perfection but because the offering was to reflect intentionality, preparation, and honor. God loves when we take our role seriously. Sloppiness doesn't glorify Him. David understood this when he said, "I will not offer to the Lord that which costs me nothing" (2 Samuel 24:24). Excellence, in its purest form, is about value—what is God worth to me?

But there's a stark difference between giving God our best and never feeling good enough. The former springs from love. The latter is rooted in fear.

Perfectionism, unlike excellence, is a cruel taskmaster. It demands performance over presence. It's the voice that says, "You missed that note; you ruined the moment." It's what silences the timid, crushes creativity, and glorifies the spotlight over the Spirit.

Jesus never scolded people for not being technically perfect in their worship. But He did confront hearts that were proud, performative, or self-righteous. He praised the widow with two mites, not because her gift was impressive, but because it was sincere and sacrificial (Mark 12:41-44).

**The Heart Behind the Offering**

Let me introduce you to Rachel.

Rachel was a worship vocalist at a church in Bangalore. She had an angelic voice—trained, confident, expressive. But she was slowly being crushed by the invisible weight of perfection. Every Sunday, she analyzed her performance—each note, each harmony. If she made one mistake, it stayed with her all week.

One evening, after leading worship at a women's retreat, Rachel locked herself in the bathroom and wept. Why? Because she had cracked on the final note of the closing song. She believed she had let God down. But that night, an older woman

approached her and said, "When you sang, I felt God lift the shame I've carried for years. Thank you."
Rachel's cracked note didn't cancel the anointing. Her heart carried the oil, not her technique.
Perfection tries to impress people. Worship seeks to bless God and minister to others.

**Jesus and the Imperfect Offering**

The Gospel of John tells the story of Mary breaking her alabaster jar and pouring perfume on Jesus' feet (John 12:1-8). That moment wasn't choreographed. It wasn't refined or rehearsed. It was raw. Costly. Overflowing. The fragrance filled the room—and so did the scandal.
Judas sneered. Others may have judged. But Jesus called it beautiful.
Why? Because the heart behind it mattered more than the presentation.
In worship leadership, we must fight to protect this sacred understanding: it is possible to be technically excellent and still spiritually dry. But when we are spiritually full, even our technical shortcomings can still carry the fragrance of Jesus.

**Encouraging Excellence the Right Way**

Excellence is not a standard of flawlessness—it's a posture of honor. It says, "Lord, I value You enough to prepare, to practice, to plan, to improve." We are stewards of a holy moment, and we should not treat it casually.
At Elevate Church in Chandigarh, the worship team led by a man, developed a beautiful weekly rhythm: they met every Friday night not just to rehearse musically, but to pray, seek Scripture, and share one way they were growing. Excellence was pursued—

but in a culture of grace, encouragement, and spiritual hunger.

This person often reminded his team, "We rehearse not to perform better, but to remove distractions so that people can encounter Jesus more clearly."

That mindset transformed everything. People didn't rehearse out of fear—they rehearsed out of reverence.

**Taming the Ego and Healing Insecurity**

Perfectionism is often a mask—sometimes hiding insecurity, sometimes feeding ego.

Some team members may struggle with feeling "not good enough." Others may secretly crave applause. Both are traps. Both miss the point.

Paul, in 1 Corinthians 12, paints a beautiful picture of the body of Christ—different parts, same Spirit, same purpose. The eye cannot say to the hand, "I don't need you." Neither can the foot say, "I don't belong." Every part matters. In worship, the same principle applies.

I recall a guitarist named Joel who, though highly skilled, constantly sought validation. He needed to be Seen. Heard. Praised. One day, after a heartfelt message about pride and brokenness, Joel shared with the team: "I've been trying to prove my worth through my playing. I want to worship, not just perform."

From that day, something shifted. Joel didn't play with less skill—he played with more surrender. And the atmosphere changed.

As leaders, we must gently guide our teams to this realization: you don't need to be perfect to be powerful. You need to be available and yielded.

**Creating a Culture Where Growth is Celebrated**

Mistakes will happen. A mic will die. Someone will start in the wrong key. The tech will fail. But these are not tragedies. These are opportunities for grace and growth.

Create an environment where people aren't afraid to try, to stretch, and even to stumble. Celebrate improvement, not just accomplishment. Applaud courage, not just perfection.

At one church I attended, the team had what they called "The Grace Bell." Anytime someone made a mistake during rehearsal and handled it with humility and humor, they got to ring the bell. It wasn't to mock—it was to remind everyone that we are all growing, and grace abounds. That small tradition diffused tension and built community.

**Excellence Is Worship—Perfectionism Is Pressure**

Let's return to the heart of it all.

God deserves our best—not because He needs it, but because we love Him. But He never demanded perfection. If that were the case, no worship team would ever qualify.

Our calling is not to impress. It is to offer. And in the offering, when done with joy and sincerity, God is glorified—even if a chord is missed or a word is forgotten.

He looks beyond the melody and into the motive.

So strive for excellence—but let it be a dance, not a duty. Let it be a gift, not a performance. And remember, sometimes, the most powerful moments come when things fall apart—and God shows up anyway.

*Because He's not waiting for your perfection. He's waiting for your yes.*

# Part II:
# Motivating and Engaging the Congregation

# Chapter 8: Understanding the Heart of the Congregation

There's something sacred about standing before a congregation, guitar in hand, or at the keyboard, ready to lead people into the presence of God. It's a humbling moment every single time. But for the worship leader who only focuses on the stage and the sound and forgets the *souls in the seats*, it can become just another performance.

We're not just leading *songs*. We're leading *people*. And people come with stories, expectations, wounds, backgrounds, and beliefs. They come with silent prayers tucked deep in their hearts, and sometimes with defenses built over years of disappointment or disconnection.

To lead them well, we must take time to know them—not just as an audience—but as a flock. That's what Jesus did.

**Jesus Knew the Crowd and the One**

Throughout the Gospels, we see Jesus' extraordinary ability to know the crowd *and* the individual. He taught thousands on the hillside—but He also noticed the widow giving her two small coins. He knew the hunger of the 5,000, and He felt the desperation of one woman who touched the hem of His garment in faith.

He understood both the *collective longing* and the *personal ache*.

Worship leaders are invited into a similar sensitivity. It's not just about preparing a great set list; it's about preparing a spiritual journey for a specific people—your people.

**Knowing Your People: Styles, History, Expectations**

Let me tell you about a church in Coimbatore where a young worship leader named Kevin had just been appointed. Kevin was passionate, talented, and full of vision. He introduced new songs, spontaneous worship, and free-flowing sets. But within weeks, murmurs grew. Some older members stopped participating. The younger ones loved it, but the congregation felt split.

Kevin was crushed. “But I’m giving my best to God,” he said.

That’s when his pastor took him aside and gently asked, “Have you taken time to understand *why* they worship the way they do?”

Kevin paused. He hadn’t. He had brought his *style*, but not his *understanding*.

Over the next few months, Kevin visited homes, had coffee with older members, talked to long-time ushers, and began to listen. He discovered that the church had a deep-rooted history of hymn-based worship, shaped by decades of missionary influence. For many, those hymns weren’t just songs—they were anchors during personal storms.

So Kevin did something radical. He created blended worship sets—modern choruses built around classic hymns. He honored the past while gently ushering in the future.

Something beautiful happened. The spiritual tension in the room lifted. Hands that had once been folded were now raised. Eyes that were once skeptical softened.

Why? Because Kevin took time to *understand the heart of his people*.

Every congregation has a worship story. And wise worship leaders honor that story even as they lead people into new expressions.

**Breaking the Consumer Mindset**

In today's world, churches—especially larger ones—can easily fall into the trap of offering a "worship experience" that feels more like a concert than a corporate encounter with God. Lights, production, perfection—none of these are evil, but they can subtly shift worship from *participation* to *observation*. The congregation becomes spectators rather than worshippers.

One Sunday, a woman named Anita approached her worship leader and said, "Worship was great today! It gave me chills!" Her excitement was genuine—but the worship leader, Rajiv, later reflected, "What if we're just giving people *spiritual goosebumps* instead of helping them offer themselves as a living sacrifice?"

That's when he changed his vocabulary. Instead of asking his team, "How was worship today?" he started asking, "Did we *equip people* to meet with God today?"

Paul's instruction in Romans 12:1 is clear: "Offer your bodies as a living sacrifice, holy and pleasing to God—this is your true and proper worship."

Worship is not a product we consume; it's a posture we assume.

To break the consumer mindset, worship leaders must model vulnerability, invite engagement, and remind the congregation that worship is not for them—it's for God. And yet, when it is truly for God, the people are deeply fulfilled. Because we were created for it.

**Discerning Spiritual Temperature**

In Revelation 2 and 3, Jesus addresses seven churches. To each, He offers a personalized message. He knows their strengths, their struggles, their spiritual temperature. He praises, corrects, warns, and invites them to return to their first love.

This is worship leadership at its most profound—seeing the spiritual condition of the people you serve and responding appropriately.

You can't do this without prayer. You can't do this without intercession. And you certainly can't do this from the green room.

To discern the temperature of a congregation, a worship leader must be *present*—in the lobby, in small groups, in prayer meetings, in people's lives.

I once knew a worship pastor named Lydia who would come to the sanctuary 30 minutes before the service and simply sit in the back row, praying over the people as they arrived. She wasn't checking lights or rehearsing transitions—she was asking the Holy Spirit: "What's the burden in the room today? What do You want to say to Your people?"

One morning, she sensed a deep heaviness. That morning, she led the team to switch the set list entirely, focusing on the faithfulness of God and His nearness in suffering. People wept. A woman who had just lost her job said, "It felt like the entire set was written for me."

That's the fruit of spiritual discernment.

### Learning the Rhythm of the Room

Sometimes, a congregation is quiet because they're reverent. Sometimes, they're quiet because they're weary. And sometimes, they're just unfamiliar with how to respond.

A worship leader's job isn't to manipulate energy—it's to *listen for the wind* and hoist the sails. Jesus said in John 3:8 that the Spirit is like the wind—you don't know where it comes from or where it's going, but you feel it. Worship leadership is part art, part surrender, and part shepherding.

You're not just playing songs—you're helping people *move*. From distraction to attention. From heaviness to hope. From self-focus to God-focus.

This requires wisdom. This requires patience. But most of all, it requires love.

### The Shepherd's Heart

In Ezekiel 34, God rebukes the shepherds of Israel who fed themselves but neglected the flock. They didn't strengthen the weak, heal the sick, bind up the injured, or bring back the strays. God's heart breaks for leaders who forget their people.

Let it not be so with us.

Let us be worship leaders who know our people—not just their voices, but their hearts. Let us lead not just with music but with mercy. Let us offer not just good songs, but sacred space for encounter, healing, and transformation.

*Because when we understand the heart of the congregation, we don't just lead worship. We lead people to the heart of God.*

# Chapter 9: Leading with Clarity, Passion, and Purpose

There's something almost electric about the moment just before worship begins. The lights may be dimming, the first chords strummed, the air thick with expectation. But beneath all the sound and stage elements, one thing ultimately determines what happens next: leadership.

Worship leadership isn't about performance. It's not about stage presence or vocal acrobatics. It's about leading people—real people—into real encounters with a real God. And to do that well, a worship leader must lead with clarity, passion, and purpose.

These three elements form a kind of sacred triad. Take away one, and the whole structure falters. Let's explore how they unfold practically and spiritually.

**Clarity: Leading Without Confusion**

Picture this: a worship team begins with a high-energy praise song, immediately transitions to a slow spontaneous moment with no clear direction, then jumps into a fast hymn without preparation. The band is tight. The vocals are strong. But the congregation is confused, unsure whether to clap, sit, sing, or listen.

This happens more often than we'd like to admit—not because of bad intentions, but because of unclear flow and direction.

In 1 Corinthians 14:33, Paul says, *"For God is not a God of confusion but of peace."* This passage, while referring to order in the early church gatherings, has clear implications for worship today: worship should make it easier—not harder—for people to engage with God.

Great worship leadership is not about showing off musical brilliance—it's about removing obstacles between the people and the Presence.

Let's take the example of Anita, a young worship leader in Pune. She was musically gifted but often felt pressure to make worship sets "spontaneous and Spirit-led." What ended up happening was lots of awkward transitions and unexplained moments that left her congregation disconnected. Her mentor lovingly told her, "Being Spirit-led doesn't mean being unprepared. God can work through structure too."

That shifted everything for Anita. She began to thoughtfully prepare her transitions. Instead of randomly jumping between songs, she prayed and asked, *What journey do You want to take our people on this Sunday?* Her worship sets became like well-plotted paths, each song a step deeper into God's heart. The atmosphere in the room changed—not because she added more songs, but because she led with clarity.

**Passion: Not Just Volume, but Fire**

Passion isn't volume. Passion isn't sweat. Passion is presence—your full heart, alive and engaged, bringing others along with you.

In Luke 24:32, after the resurrected Jesus walks with the disciples on the road to Emmaus, they say, *"Were not our hearts burning within us while he talked with us on the road?"* That's passion. Not noise, but fire. Not hype, but heat.

When a worship leader is truly passionate about God—when every word they sing flows from deep love—it's contagious. You can't manufacture that. You can't fake it. And you certainly can't replace it with lights or reverb.

I remember watching a worship leader named Joshua in a small village church. He wasn't classically trained. His guitar was missing a string. But when he sang, "Great is Thy faithfulness," you could *feel* the years of pain, trust, and dependence behind every word. He sang like someone who knew what it meant to need God for every breath.

His passion wasn't performance—it was born in the furnace of real life. And it led his congregation into *real* worship.

**Purpose: Knowing Why You're There**

Purpose gives your leadership weight. It answers the question: *Why are we doing this?*

Every song should be chosen on purpose. Every transition should serve a purpose. Every word spoken from the platform should lead people *toward* something, not just fill time.

David, the shepherd king, was a man of deep purpose in worship. He didn't just sing psalms because they sounded nice. He sang them because they were the overflow of a heart gripped by God. In Psalm 27:4, he writes, *"One thing I ask from the Lord... that I may dwell in the house of the Lord all the days of my life."* One thing. One purpose.

As worship leaders, our purpose is to glorify God and to help people connect to Him personally and corporately.

Take the story of Priya, who led worship at a large city church. She used to think her role was to set the "spiritual mood" before the preacher took the stage. But over time, through mentorship and Scripture, she came to understand worship as more than a prelude. It was a meeting place. Her goal shifted from "filling the time" to "facilitating encounter." Her leadership became weightier—not heavy, but rooted.

Purpose pulls people out of the routine and into revelation.

**Short Exhortations That Lead, Not Preach**

A powerful tool in worship leadership is the short exhortation—those in-between-song moments where a leader can share a Scripture, a prayer, or a brief encouragement. But here's the key: these moments must *serve the moment*, not hijack it.

In Acts 2, Peter's speech after Pentecost was brief, focused, and cut to the heart. Likewise, our exhortations during worship must be anchored in Scripture, timely, and Spirit-led.

Let's say you're transitioning from a song about surrender into one about God's power. Instead of saying, "Now let's sing another song," a leader could say:

*"Church, as we lay our burdens down before Him, let's remember who we're giving them to. Isaiah 40:29 says, 'He gives strength to the weary and increases the power of the weak.' He is not only worthy—He is able. Let's worship Him with that in mind."*

It's simple. It's Scripture. It's intentional. And it prepares hearts to sing with meaning, not just melody.

**Avoiding Hype: Choosing Heart Over Hysteria**

Let's be honest. In an age of viral moments, it's tempting to turn worship into an emotional high. But emotion doesn't always equal transformation. People can cry in a concert and walk away unchanged. God desires not hype, but heart change.

In the story of Elijah on Mount Horeb (1 Kings 19), God wasn't in the wind, earthquake, or fire. He came in a gentle whisper. Sometimes the most life-changing moments in worship aren't the loud ones, but the still ones.

Leaders must resist the urge to manufacture moments. Trust the Holy Spirit. If there's silence, don't rush to fill it. If there's weeping, don't interrupt it. And if there's stillness, don't panic. Some of the deepest transformation happens in stillness.

### The Role of Vulnerability and Authenticity on Stage

Finally, and perhaps most powerfully, worship leaders must be real.

Not perfect. Not polished. Not ultra-spiritual. Just *real*.

Jesus didn't hide His emotions. He wept. He was moved with compassion. He sweat blood in the garden. And through it all, He worshipped with a heart aligned to the Father.

When worship leaders are vulnerable, it invites others to bring their true selves to God too. You don't have to share every personal struggle from the mic, but when your worship is born from real dependence, people know.

Take Ruth, a worship leader in Hyderabad who had just gone through a miscarriage. When she led worship a few weeks later, she didn't give a speech. She didn't even explain. But as she softly sang, "You are good, good, oh," the tears streamed down her face.

She was raw. She was real. And the room responded. People realized—*worship doesn't deny pain; it brings it before God.* That morning, dozens encountered the comfort of the Holy Spirit in a way no perfectly executed song set ever could.

**Lead Like Jesus Would**

To lead with clarity, passion, and purpose is to lead like Jesus.

He was clear in His teaching. He was passionate in His love. He was purposeful in every step.

He didn't manipulate. He didn't perform. He *led.* Boldly. Gently. Authentically.

And that's your call too.

So when you step onto the stage, let your heart be right. Let your focus be sharp. Let your voice be real. And let your purpose be anchored in this one thing: that Jesus would be seen, known, and worshipped.

*And if you lead that way, no matter how simple or grand the moment, the heavens will open, and hearts will be changed.*

# Chapter 10:
# Creating Space for Encounter

Worship is not just about music; it's about meeting. A meeting between heaven and earth. Between the divine and the dusty. Between the Creator and His created.

But for that meeting to take place, someone must make room—to pause, to breathe, to wait. That's what this chapter is about: *creating space for encounter.*

Not every moment in worship needs to be filled with sound. Not every song needs to be polished. Sometimes, what people really need is not more music, but a moment of stillness where their hearts can catch up with God's voice.

Let's walk through how we can become worship leaders who don't just fill time—but host Presence.

**Less Performance, More Presence**

There's a fine line between excellence and performance—and crossing that line is easy in today's worship culture.

Lights, loops, transitions, click tracks, vocal stacks—it can all become a show if we're not careful. But the Kingdom is not impressed with production value. God isn't after our perfection; He's after our presence. He wants us *with* Him and invites us to lead others into the same.

King David understood this deeply. He was a skilled musician, yes—but when the ark of the covenant returned to Jerusalem in 2 Samuel 6, David didn't lead with performance. He danced with abandon. He was clothed not in regalia, but in a linen ephod—

common, humble. He worshipped with everything, *without concern for appearance.*

Michal, his wife, despised him for it. But David replied, *"I will become even more undignified than this."* Why? Because God was there. And when God is in the room, we don't perform—we participate.

I recall the story of a worship leader named Thomas in Bangalore. He had a powerful voice, perfect pitch, and flawless command of his band. People admired his sets—but they often left unchanged. One day, during a midweek prayer meeting, his guitar string snapped. No band. No backup. Just him and a roomful of people. He simply whispered, "Let's wait on God."

There was no music—just silence. And in that silence, someone began to weep. Then another. Then another. The Holy Spirit began to minister, not through a song, but through *stillness*. That night, lives were touched in ways no full setlist ever had.

Thomas later said, "It was the most powerful worship I ever led—and I never sang a note." That's the power of presence over performance.

### The Sacred Power of Silence, Spontaneity, and Invitation

We live in a world afraid of silence. We fill every gap with noise. But in worship, silence isn't empty. It's sacred.

In Revelation 8:1, there is a curious verse: *"When he opened the seventh seal, there was silence in heaven for about half an hour."* Think about that—heaven, the place of unceasing worship, pauses in reverence. Silence isn't absence; it's awareness. It creates space for God to speak.

Sometimes, as worship leaders, we're afraid of the quiet. We think people will grow restless. We fear awkwardness. But often, those pauses are the very place where hearts start listening.

And then there's spontaneity—those unplanned, unscripted moments where the Holy Spirit stirs something that wasn't in the setlist.

Let's look at Paul and Silas in Acts 16. Locked in prison, beaten and bound, they began to sing—not because it was scheduled, but because their hearts needed to. That spontaneous praise *shook the foundations* of the prison. Doors opened. Chains fell. Worship didn't just comfort them—it *broke through* the natural and released the supernatural.

As worship leaders, we must leave space for those moments. A spontaneous chorus. A new melody. A prophetic word. Sometimes, it's not about what's next in the song list—it's about what's next in the Spirit.

Then there's invitation—the gentle, Spirit-led act of saying, *"Come."* Come forward if you need healing. Come sit if you need rest. Come open your heart to the Lord. This isn't manipulation—it's *facilitation*. Jesus often extended invitations, not commands. *"Come to me, all you who are weary."* He didn't shout. He didn't hype. He simply opened the door.

A young worship leader named Leya in Kochi once felt the Lord prompting her to stop mid-set and say, "If you've been struggling with depression, Jesus wants to comfort you tonight." She almost ignored it—thinking it was too personal, too risky. But she obeyed.

Five people came forward. One was on the brink of suicide that night. The worship didn't just entertain—it rescued. All because someone paused to listen and made room for an invitation.

**Allowing the Holy Spirit to Lead**

This is perhaps the most crucial—and most difficult—part of worship leadership: *not being the leader.*

Letting the Holy Spirit take the lead means releasing control. It means planning, yes—but holding those plans with open hands. It means knowing that one whisper from God is worth more than ten perfectly executed songs.

In John 3:8, Jesus says, *"The wind blows wherever it pleases. You hear its sound, but you cannot tell where it comes from or where it is going."* That's how the Spirit works. We don't control the wind—we set our sails and follow it.

Allowing the Holy Spirit to lead is not an excuse for laziness or lack of preparation. On the contrary, it requires *deep preparation*—both musically and spiritually—so that when He moves, we are ready to move with Him.

I think of Reuben, a worship leader at a large multicultural church in Chennai. His team rehearsed meticulously each week. Every moment timed. Every transition scripted. But one Sunday, during the third song, he felt the Lord prompting him to stop. Not to play. Not to sing. Just to wait.

It was uncomfortable. Unscripted. But in that stillness, someone began to cry. Then another. Suddenly, one of the backup singers felt led to pray over the mic. It wasn't planned. But the presence of God flooded the room like a tide breaking through a dam.

Reuben's only role that day was to *get out of the way*. He didn't need to finish the setlist. The Spirit had taken over—and the people encountered God for themselves.

**Becoming a Door, Not a Destination**

As worship leaders, we are not the destination. We are the doorway.

Our job is not to get people to admire us—but to usher them into the throne room. To create a space so uncluttered, so open, so yielded, that God Himself can move freely.

We are gatekeepers. Hosts. Carriers of presence. Not performers.

When we prioritize presence over perfection, invitation over instruction, and surrender over control, we become like the curtain in the temple—torn open so others can step into the Holy of Holies.

*So the next time you lead, remember: you don't need to do everything. You just need to create space—and God will do the rest.*

*Make room. Let go. And watch Him come.*

# Chapter 11:
# Teaching the Theology of Worship

There comes a moment in every worship leader's journey when they realize something sobering: it's possible to have a church that sings loudly but still doesn't truly worship.

Week after week, songs are sung, hands lifted, emotions stirred—but without a real understanding of what worship actually *is*, the people remain at the *surface* while God is inviting them into the *deep*.

That's why we must teach worship. Not just lead it. We must disciple the congregation into understanding that worship is not a genre, not a feeling, not a Sunday activity—it is a life offered to God in awe, love, and obedience. Worship is not just music; it's theology in motion.

And the church desperately needs that theology back.

**The First Song Wasn't Sung—It Was Lived**

Worship began long before the first chord was strummed or the first psalm was penned. It began in Genesis.

Before there was an altar, there was *a walk in the garden*. Adam walked with God in the cool of the day. That was worship—unbroken fellowship. It wasn't ceremonial. It wasn't corporate. It was relational.

When sin broke that intimacy, God began unfolding a story of redemption where worship became the pathway back into His presence. From Abel's acceptable offering to Abraham's willing sacrifice of Isaac, from the Tabernacle of Moses to the Psalms of David, worship was never about music—it was about the heart.

Jesus made this crystal clear in John 4 when He met the Samaritan woman at the well. She tried to spark a theological debate: *"Our ancestors worshiped on this mountain, but you Jews claim the place to worship is Jerusalem."* But Jesus cut through the noise.

*"A time is coming when you will worship the Father neither on this mountain nor in Jerusalem… true worshipers will worship the Father in Spirit and in truth."*

This was radical. Worship was no longer about *place*—it was about *posture*.

**Educating the Congregation: A Mission, Not a Moment**

If worship is meant to be "in spirit and truth," then truth must be taught.

One of the most powerful things a worship leader or pastor can do is to regularly *teach* on worship—not in hour-long sermons necessarily, but through consistent, Spirit-filled 5-minute teachings before or after a worship set.

It could be as simple as saying:

"This morning, as we sing, remember that worship isn't just about how we feel—it's about who God is. Even if you're tired or distracted, you can offer your heart to Him today."

Or:

"Psalm 100 says to *enter His gates with thanksgiving*. Let's not wait until we *feel* God—we'll thank Him first, and trust that He'll meet us here."

One pastor I knew of from Hyderabad, would take two minutes every Sunday before the first note played and teach the congregation a single worship truth. Over a year, the church learned about the Tabernacle pattern of worship, the sacrifice of praise, the difference between thanksgiving, praise, and worship, and how the Psalms were actually *training manuals* for the soul.

Soon, the atmosphere changed. People weren't just singing; they were *responding with revelation*. That's what theology does—it gives meaning to the music.

### Worship as a Lifestyle, Not Just a Sunday Soundtrack

We've unintentionally trained people to view worship as a Sunday morning setlist. But God is not looking for a weekly audience—He's seeking *daily altars*.

Romans 12:1 reminds us of this:

*"Therefore, I urge you, brothers and sisters, in view of God's mercy, to offer your bodies as a living sacrifice, holy and pleasing to God—this is your true and proper worship."*

What is worship? A life laid down.

- ✓ When a teenager forgives a friend who wronged them, that's worship.
- ✓ When a businessman refuses to cut corners in a deal, that's worship.
- ✓ When a mother changes a diaper with patience and sings over her child, heaven calls that worship.

True worship is not just expressed in melody—it's expressed in *obedience*.

We need to begin reminding our congregations: "Worship doesn't end when the band stops playing. It begins when you walk out the door."

One young man, Asher, once shared how he started seeing his 9-to-5 job as an act of worship after a message series on Romans 12. He said, "I realized that if I did my work with excellence, with a heart to glorify God and bless my coworkers, I was worshiping—even without singing." That revelation transformed his joy and purpose.

**Short Teachings, Long Impact**

You don't need an hour to shape theology. You need consistency.

Start by planning short, powerful truths into your worship gatherings. Pair them with Scripture. Make them repeatable. Let people *soak* in the truth week after week.

For example:

Before a song about surrender, share the story of Abraham offering Isaac.

Before a song of victory, remind them of Paul and Silas singing in prison.

Before communion, teach how worship is not only upward (toward God) but also inward (changing us) and outward (loving others).

Jesus often taught in brief, rich truths. "Where your treasure is, there your heart will be also." That single line has shaped centuries of believers.

Use your platform wisely—sow seeds of truth, not just sound.

**Encouraging Personal Worship During the Week**

The greatest indicator of a church's worship health is not the Sunday volume—it's the *Monday silence*.

If people are only engaging God through corporate worship, they're missing 90% of the relationship. We must teach them how to worship personally: in the car, in the kitchen, in the quiet.

Encourage them to:

- ✓ Put on worship music while doing chores.
- ✓ Take a verse and turn it into a personal prayer.
- ✓ Journal one thing God did each day and thank Him for it.
- ✓ Sing even if they feel out of tune—because God listens to *hearts*, not harmonies.

A young woman named Rina once shared with her church that she began setting aside 10 minutes every morning just to sing to God softly before the day began. No fancy keyboard. No worship team. Just her voice and His presence.

She said, "It's like the air in my home changed. I walk lighter. My kids notice I smile more. I thought worship needed a band. I now know it just needs a willing heart."

**Reclaiming Worship from Culture, Returning It to the King**

The modern church often mirrors culture. But true worship doesn't copy the world—it consecrates us to God.

When we teach worship biblically, we reclaim it from consumerism, from personality-driven experiences, from emotional highs that fade by Sunday night. We return it to the heart of what it is: *loving God with all our heart, soul, mind, and strength*.

Let your worship ministry not only sound beautiful—but speak truth.

Let it not only lead people in songs—but lead them to surrender.

Let it raise not just hands—but living sacrifices.

*Because in the end, worship that is not taught… is often not caught.*

*But worship that is understood, lived, and loved—becomes a flame that cannot be quenched.*

# Chapter 12: Breaking Through Barriers to Worship

Every Sunday, people walk through the church doors carrying invisible weights. Some are wearing smiles, but behind those expressions are hearts battling spiritual fatigue, mental distractions, emotional wounds, or even silent rebellion. They gather with others to sing, to pray, and to hear God's Word—but a surprising number of them remain disengaged.

They stand in the sanctuary, yet feel distant from the presence of God.

This isn't because they're unspiritual. It's because there are *barriers* to worship that must be addressed with compassion, truth, and spiritual insight.

**The Battle for the Heart**

Worship is war. It always has been.

In the Old Testament, worship was constantly contested. Pharaoh refused to let Israel go to worship in the wilderness. When they finally escaped Egypt, they built a golden calf rather than waiting on God's presence. Over and over, their hearts were tempted to turn away from the living God to idols of their own making.

In the New Testament, Jesus entered a world full of tradition but void of intimacy. The Pharisees honored God with their lips, but their hearts were far from Him (Matthew 15:8). They knew the motions but missed the Messiah.

Today, we face different idols—apathy, distraction, cultural comfort, self-importance—but the battle is the same.

Worship is the pursuit of a heart fully engaged with God. And that heart must often press through barriers to reach Him.

**Apathy: When Hearts Grow Cold**

One of the greatest enemies of worship is not hatred. It is indifference.

Apathy sneaks in when worship becomes routine. When the songs are familiar, the schedule is fixed, and no one expects anything to *change*. Slowly, people become spectators instead of participants. They begin to mouth the lyrics but disconnect from their meaning.

This is not a new issue. The prophet Malachi confronted it head-on. God said to the priests in Malachi 1:13, *"You say, 'What a burden!' and you sniff at it contemptuously... When you bring injured, lame or diseased animals and offer them as sacrifices, should I accept them from your hands?"*

God wasn't angry at their lack of sacrifice—He was grieved by their lack of *honor*.

Apathy must be addressed not with guilt, but with vision. Remind the church who God is. Stir their hearts with stories of His goodness. Sometimes apathy is broken not by rebuke, but by remembrance.

Like Pastor Daniel, a worship leader in a small village church in Tamil Nadu, who began each service by reading a one-minute testimony from someone in the church—a healed body, a restored relationship, a financial miracle. Slowly, the people came alive again. Why? Because their hearts remembered that God still moves.

**Distraction: The Noise That Drowns the Voice**

In our hyper-connected world, distraction is a daily reality. Minds are racing with to-do lists, phone notifications, family concerns, or the meal they forgot to prep. Even in the sanctuary, hearts are often elsewhere.

But distraction isn't just modern—it's biblical. In Luke 10, Martha was "distracted with much serving" while Mary sat at Jesus' feet. Martha was doing good things—but missing the best thing.

As worship leaders and pastors, we must gently guide the congregation back to the *main thing*. That means building worship sets that give space for people to slow down. Silence is not our enemy; it's an invitation to refocus.

A worship leader named Priya once shared how, instead of opening with an upbeat song, her team played soft instrumental music for 90 seconds while inviting people to close their eyes and "lay down every distraction before the Lord." The difference in atmosphere was undeniable. People who had walked in scattered became centered in God's presence.

Distraction isn't defeated with louder music—it's broken through stillness and focus.

**Discomfort: When Worship Feels Foreign**

Let's be honest—worship can feel awkward for many. Especially for first-timers, new believers, or those from non-expressive traditions. Lifting hands, singing aloud, or closing their eyes may feel unnatural or even intimidating.

David danced before the Lord with all his might (2 Samuel 6), but his wife Michal despised him in her heart. His expression of worship made her uncomfortable. And yet, it was *David* God called "a man after My own heart."

We need to normalize worship as something biblical, not cultural. Some people may resist expressive worship, believing it's "emotionalism" or reserved for the "charismatic crowd." But Scripture is full of expressive worship: clapping (Psalm 47:1), kneeling (Psalm 95:6), shouting (Psalm 100:1), even lying prostrate (2 Chronicles 20:18).

As leaders, we must model and gently explain that worship is not about performance—it's about *posture before God*.

One church in Bengaluru, when introducing new worship expressions, created a "Worship 101" mini-class after service for curious attendees. It helped bridge the gap for those who were unsure or hesitant. The result? Unity grew. Expressions diversified. And no one felt judged.

## Cultural & Generational Gaps: One Church, Many Preferences

In many congregations, especially in India and multi-ethnic churches around the world, worship tastes vary widely. The older generation may prefer hymns, while younger believers connect with modern contemporary songs. Regional language preferences may clash with English-dominated sets. The result? Frustration and detachment.

This is where the heart of *servant leadership* must shine. Worship is not about satisfying personal taste—it's about honoring God and edifying the body.

Paul addressed this in 1 Corinthians 9:22 when he said, *"I have become all things to all people so that by all possible means I might save some."* In worship, we must become *bridge builders*.

One worship team created blended sets with both classic and contemporary songs. Another alternated between languages—Tamil one week, Hindi the next, English choruses woven throughout. Unity wasn't forged by uniformity, but by humility and love.

A mature church learns that worship is not for *me*, but for *Him*.

**Shame, Pride, and Emotional Numbness**

Some people cannot worship because shame has wrapped around their heart like chains. They believe they are too unworthy, too broken, too far gone. Others are bound by pride—they fear being seen as vulnerable or "too spiritual." Some have simply gone numb, hardened by grief or prolonged disappointment.

In Luke 7, a sinful woman broke an alabaster jar and poured it over Jesus' feet. She wept. She kissed His feet. She worshipped freely. The religious leaders were disgusted, but Jesus said, *"She loved much because she was forgiven much."*

That's the kind of worship that breaks through shame and pride.

To help people overcome these barriers, we must create safe, grace-filled spaces. We must remind them that worship is not about what we've done, but what Christ has done. That His blood has given us access to the Father. That we can come boldly, no matter how broken.

Pastor Elijah, a man of quiet wisdom, once opened a service with these words:

*"Some of you feel like you're not worthy to sing today. Let me remind you: None of us are. But Jesus makes us worthy. That's why we sing—not because we're perfect, but because He is."*
Tears filled many eyes. The worship that day was not loud—but it was real.

**Praying Over the People: Preparing the Atmosphere**
One of the most overlooked weapons in breaking barriers to worship is *intercessory prayer* before the service begins.
Before instruments are tuned or slides are loaded, pray over the people. Pray for soft hearts, lifted heads, and open spirits. Pray for walls to come down and for the Holy Spirit to move freely.
Jesus often withdrew to pray before significant moments (Luke 5:16). If He, the Son of God, found power in pre-service prayer, how much more do we need it?
A worship leader named Rachel began gathering her team 20 minutes before every service to pray for the congregation. They laid hands on the seats. They prayed for healing, deliverance, joy, and revelation. Over time, they noticed a shift. People began coming in more hungry, more expectant.
The breakthrough often begins before the first note is played.

**The God Who Breaks Every Barrier**
No heart is too hard. No mind too distracted. No past too shameful.
We serve the God who tore the veil from top to bottom. The God who welcomes prodigals and

silences Pharisees. The God who turns the lukewarm into burning hearts.

As worship leaders, pastors, and believers, our role is not to *manufacture* encounters—but to *remove the barriers* that block them. Through truth, love, patience, and prayer, we prepare the way for God's presence to meet His people.

Let us believe again. Pray again. Speak life again.

Because when the barriers fall, the Bride will rise in worship—and heaven will rejoice.

# Chapter 13: Inviting Participation and Engagement

Worship isn't a concert. It's not a performance. It's a holy invitation.

When a congregation gathers for worship, we're not trying to impress them—we're trying to *include* them. Worship is not a spectator event; it's a participatory experience. God doesn't want people standing at a distance while a few people sing on a stage. He desires a people, not just a platform.

Yet, in churches around the world, week after week, many pastors and worship leaders look out at silent congregations—people mouthing lyrics half-heartedly, arms crossed, eyes wandering. The passion isn't absent because they don't love God. Often, they've simply not been invited in the right way.

So how do we change that? How do we move from performance to participation?

Let's explore the heart and art of leading people into active, engaged, transformative worship.

## The Call to Sing: From Spectators to Sons and Daughters

All through Scripture, we see that *singing* is not optional—it's a command and a joy.

In Psalm 96:1, we're told:

"Sing to the Lord a new song; sing to the Lord, all the earth."

Again and again, the Bible connects singing with worship. Not just listening. Not just attending. Singing.

Singing unites hearts, stirs the soul, and teaches truth. Paul said in Colossians 3:16:

"Let the message of Christ dwell among you richly… as you sing psalms, hymns, and spiritual songs to God with gratitude in your hearts."

That's why as worship leaders, our task isn't just to sing *at* people. It's to draw the songs out of them. To create a space where they feel comfortable, confident, and compelled to join in.

But how?

**Practical Techniques to Get People Singing**

Let's meet Arun, a young worship leader from a church in Hyderabad. He loved Jesus deeply and had a strong voice—but every Sunday, his congregation just stood there, barely moving their lips. Frustrated, Arun prayed, "Lord, what am I doing wrong?"

The Lord reminded him: *You're singing for them, not with them.*

From that moment, Arun changed his approach. He started inviting participation in small but meaningful ways—and slowly, things shifted.

Here's what Arun learned—and what every worship leader must remember:

- ✓ Begin with the Familiar: Start with a well-known song, even if it's old. Familiarity builds confidence. When people feel secure, they sing louder. Arun began every set with a song like *"How Great Thou Art"* or *"Blessed Assurance"*—and the congregation came alive.

- ✓ Simplify the Melody: Some worship leaders love complex harmonies or spontaneous modulations—but if the people can't follow, they'll stop singing. Lead clearly, stay on key, and keep it singable.
- ✓ Speak Between Songs: A short, heartfelt encouragement between songs—"Let's sing this as a prayer," or "Lift your voice with me"—can make all the difference. Sometimes the breakthrough comes through spoken invitation, not sung repetition.
- ✓ Make Eye Contact: Worship with your *face*, not just your voice. Look at the people. Smile. Worship openly. If they see your passion, it invites theirs.

**The Power of Lyrics, Visuals, and Posture**

Let's imagine a visitor—Meera, a first-time guest in church. She doesn't know the songs. She's unsure about the process. The lyrics flash on the screen, but they're delayed or misspelled. The worship leader is singing with eyes closed the entire time. Meera stands quietly, unsure what to do.

Her experience is common—and avoidable.

Clear lyrics are crucial. Use screens. Use well-timed slides. Avoid typos or late changes. What people *see* affects what they can *sing*.

Visuals matter too—not just lyrics, but the ambiance. A worship environment should be inviting, not distracting. If lights are too bright or too dark, if visuals are chaotic, it breaks focus. A clean, beautiful, intentional stage environment fosters deeper engagement.

Posture is powerful.

In the Old Testament, people bowed down, knelt, raised hands, stood in awe. Posture isn't just physical—it's spiritual. It reflects what's happening inside.

Encourage people gently. Say things like:

"If you feel comfortable, lift your hands with me as we surrender to Him."

"Let's all stand in reverence before the Lord."

Don't command—invite. Lead by example. The Spirit will do the rest.

**Call-and-Response: Ancient and Powerful**

One of the oldest forms of participatory worship is call-and-response. It's biblical, beautiful, and incredibly effective.

In Psalm 136, we see it in action:

*"Give thanks to the Lord, for He is good"*

His love endures forever.

*"Give thanks to the God of gods"*

His love endures forever.

This rhythm invites engagement. It gives people a role in the worship.

Worship leaders can use this naturally:

*"Can we say together—You are worthy, Lord!"*

*"Sing this line after me…"*

*"Let's declare this together…"*

It's especially helpful when introducing new songs.

**Introducing New Songs Effectively**

Every church needs fresh songs—but nothing kills participation faster than overwhelming the congregation with unfamiliar tunes week after week. Here's a better way.

**Introduce Slowly**

Choose one new song every few weeks. Play it as a special first. Then add it to the set the following week. Repetition breeds comfort.

**Teach It**

Before singing, take 30 seconds: *"Here's a new song. The chorus goes like this…"* Sing it once. Then invite them to join.

**Repeat It Often**

Don't drop a new song after one Sunday. Sing it consistently for a few weeks. Help it sink in.

**Connect It to Scripture**

Say, *"This song comes from Psalm 23,"* or "*It's based on Jesus' words in Matthew 11."* This gives the song depth—and reminds people it's not just melody, it's ministry.

Arun once introduced a song called "*Faithful Through the Fire."* The first time, only the worship team sang. But by the third week, the whole church sang the chorus like a battle cry. Why? Because he taught it, repeated it, and connected it to their current series on trials and testing. It became *their* song.

## Creating Anchor Songs: What the Church Can Own

Every church needs what I call anchor songs—songs that carry the church's heart. Songs that feel like home. Songs that people sing *before* the first chord is even struck.

Anchor songs are not necessarily the newest. They're the most *beloved*.

In the wilderness, Israel had a song. After crossing the Red Sea, they sang (Exodus 15), "I will sing unto the Lord, for He has triumphed gloriously!" It was their anchor song.

In Acts 16, Paul and Silas sang hymns in prison. Even chains couldn't silence their song.
What is your church's song in the fire? What song makes the walls shake with praise?
Anchor songs become part of your community's spiritual DNA. They create unity across generations, languages, and cultures.
One church had a song called "My Jesus is Enough." It was written by someone in the congregation. It was simple, powerful, and became their anthem. Every time they sang it, tears would fall, hands would lift, and hearts would rise. It wasn't just a song—it was a shared testimony.
Find those songs. Sing them often. Let them echo in the hallways, homes, and hearts of your people.

**The Joy of Shared Worship**
The goal is not just musical excellence—it is congregational engagement. Worship is most powerful when everyone sings. When voices rise as one. When hearts align. When heaven hears not one voice—but a multitude.
Let's not lead like soloists. Let's lead like shepherds—guiding people into the pasture of praise, the still waters of worship, and the open field of God's presence.
Let us say with David:
*"Come, let us sing for joy to the Lord; let us shout aloud to the Rock of our salvation."* (Psalm 95:1)
Because when the church *sings together*, walls fall, hearts heal, and God is glorified.

# Chapter 14: Consistency in Leading People to Jesus

At the very heart of worship, there must always be Jesus.
Not the music.
Not the moment.
Not the mood.
Jesus.
Every worship set, every chord played, every lyric sung, every breath taken on that platform must be aimed like an arrow to the throne of the risen King. Worship is not about ambiance; it's about adoration. Not about aesthetics; it's about allegiance. And unless we are intentionally pointing people to the person of Christ, we're just orchestrating religious concerts.
The church does not need more performers. The church needs more pointers—people who faithfully, consistently, week after week, set their eyes on Jesus and say, "Come, let me show you the One who saved my soul."
Let's explore what it means to consistently lead people to Jesus—not occasionally, not accidentally, but purposefully and passionately every single time we stand before God's people.

**Keeping Jesus at the Center of Every Set**
There's a temptation that many worship leaders—often unknowingly—fall into. The temptation to build a set around themes, trends, or technical brilliance, while the central focus quietly drifts away from Christ.

Think of it like this: a beautifully wrapped gift box, perfectly tied with a ribbon, but when opened—empty.

Jesus is not a garnish we sprinkle on top of a set. He is the meal. He is not the afterthought. He is the Alpha and the Omega, the beginning, the middle, and the end of worship.

When planning your set, ask yourself:

*Is this song magnifying Jesus?*

*Are we lifting up His name or just stirring emotions?*

*Could someone attend our service and never truly encounter Christ?*

In John 12:32, Jesus declared,

*"And I, when I am lifted up from the earth, will draw all people to myself."*

That principle still holds. Exalt Jesus, and people will be drawn.

Let's take the example of Grace Community Church, where a worship leader named Joel noticed something odd. Their worship was technically perfect—on pitch, on tempo, on time. But something felt missing. After service, he rarely heard anyone talk about Jesus. They'd say, "The music was awesome!" or "That guitar solo was amazing!"

Convicted, Joel began shifting the focus of their worship planning. They started choosing songs that explicitly named and glorified Jesus. He began every worship set by reading a gospel verse and declaring who Jesus is.

In time, the culture changed. Testimonies began flowing in—people spoke of encounters, not just impressions. Worship became revelation, not just repetition.

Worship without Christ is a building without foundation. It may stand for a moment, but it cannot last.

**Guarding the Worship Experience from Becoming a Performance**

We live in a performance-driven culture. Everywhere we look, there's a stage, a screen, a show. And if we're not vigilant, that mindset will seep into our sanctuaries.

There's nothing wrong with excellence. God deserves our best. But excellence must never overshadow intimacy. When the spotlight becomes brighter than the cross, we've lost our way.

Let's go back to 2 Samuel 6. David, the king, danced before the Lord "with all his might." There were instruments, shouts, celebration. But David wasn't performing—he was worshiping.

Now contrast that with the New Testament Pharisees, who Jesus said "do all their deeds to be seen by others" (Matthew 23:5). Their robes were fine. Their prayers were long. But their hearts were cold.

Worship isn't about being seen. It's about becoming invisible—so that Jesus may be seen more clearly.

Let me share the story of Anita, a backup vocalist in a small church in Kerala. She was gifted, classically trained, and often took solos. But one day, her pastor pulled her aside and asked gently, "Are you worshiping or performing?" It stung—but it struck deep.

That week, Anita prayed, "Jesus, let my voice disappear if You're not being glorified." And something changed. Her singing didn't become less beautiful—it became anointed. People said they felt drawn to Jesus when she sang, not just impressed by her skill. She had crossed over from performance to presence.

**Celebrating Testimonies of Worship Impact**

Worship doesn't just honor God—it also changes lives. And those stories need to be told.

In the Gospel of John, chapter 4, the woman at the well encountered Jesus and immediately became a witness. "Come, see a man..." she told the whole town. Her worship became her testimony.

Every church has stories like these—but too often, they're left untold.

As leaders, we must create space to share these moments. When someone says, "I felt the love of God during that song," or "I cried through the whole worship," don't just smile and move on. Pause. Rejoice. Share. Celebrate.

At Hope City Fellowship, Pastor Daniel made it a habit to ask for worship testimonies at the end of every month. One woman shared how the song "Jesus at the Center" had carried her through chemotherapy. Another man said he encountered Jesus for the first time while singing "What a Beautiful Name."

These weren't just songs. They were invitations to transformation.

When we celebrate what Jesus does through worship, it reminds people that this is not just music—it's ministry.

**Never Assuming People Know What Worship Is**

Let's never forget this: every week, someone walks into our church who has no idea what worship is.

Maybe they were invited by a friend. Maybe they're visiting from another faith. Maybe they've known religion their whole life, but never had a personal relationship with Jesus.

We must not assume. We must always invite.

Jesus never assumed. When He saw the crowds, He taught them, welcomed them, explained the Kingdom of God patiently and passionately.

As worship leaders, we must do the same. A simple phrase like:

"If this is new to you, welcome. We're so glad you're here. Worship is just us turning our hearts toward Jesus—feel free to observe, or join in as you're ready."

These words disarm fear. They open the door. And when people feel safe, they're more likely to step in.

I recall a story from Pastor Victor, who led a small congregation in Tamil Nadu. One Sunday, a young man named Karthik walked in—a skeptic, an atheist, a friend of a church member. During the first song, Karthik stood stiffly. But Pastor Victor, from the mic, gently said, "Worship is our response to a God who loves us. You're welcome here, whether you sing or just listen."

That invitation melted walls. By the end of the service, Karthik was in tears. Months later, he got saved—and became part of the worship team himself.

Never underestimate the power of invitation.

**Consistency is the Key**

Here's the truth: anyone can lead one great worship set.

But consistency—that's the mark of a servant, not a star.

The people in your church may forget what you wore. They may not remember every song. But they'll remember how faithfully you pointed them to Jesus.
Week after week. Month after month. Year after year.
It's not about flash. It's about faithfulness.
Whether five people or five hundred are in the room, whether the sound is flawless or falling apart—point to Jesus. Every time. Without fail.

**In Closing: A Prayer for Consistent Leaders**

*Lord Jesus,*
*We commit ourselves again to You.*
*Let our worship be centered on You, not ourselves.*
*Let our voices rise to magnify You—not to be admired.*
*Let every note, every lyric, every chord be like incense before Your throne.*
*Help us to lead not with hype, but with holiness.*
*May our ministry be marked not by performance, but by Your presence.*
*Not by applause, but by anointing.*
*And may we never grow tired of leading people to You.*
*Week after week, may Your name be lifted high—until the day when every tongue confesses and every knee bows before You.*
*In Your name we worship,*
*Amen.*

# Part III:

## Sustaining a Culture of Worship

# Chapter 15: Worship Beyond the Platform

When the lights go down…
When the mics are switched off…
When the stage is empty and the sanctuary is quiet…
Worship must continue.

Because true worship was never meant to be contained by a platform, or restricted to 30 minutes on a Sunday. Worship was never meant to be confined to melodies, harmonies, and sound systems. Worship is life. It is who we are before it is ever what we do.

The apostle Paul captures it beautifully in Romans 12:1:

*"Therefore, I urge you, brothers and sisters, in view of God's mercy, to offer your bodies as a living sacrifice, holy and pleasing to God—this is your true and proper worship."*

He didn't say, *"Offer your voice."*
He didn't say, *"Offer your songs."*
He said, *"Offer your bodies."*

In other words, worship is the life we live in response to the One we love.

As worship leaders, team members, and believers, our greatest calling is not just to lead songs—but to lead lives that glorify Jesus. And to create and sustain a culture where everyone in our churches understands this truth.

Let's explore what it looks like when worship flows beyond the platform and into every corner of our lives, our homes, our small groups, our offices, and our cities.

**Fostering a Worship Lifestyle in Your Team and Church**

Let's begin where it matters most—the worship team itself.

If the team on stage sees worship only as a task or a time slot, they'll lead with their talent, not with their testimony. And that difference is massive.

Worship is caught more than it is taught. If the team is worshiping during the week, it will overflow on Sundays. If they're not, then no amount of rehearsal can fake that intimacy.

Let me introduce you to Ethan, a keyboardist at More Grace Church. Technically brilliant, he never missed a practice. But over time, his leader noticed something—Ethan wasn't showing up spiritually. He was playing the notes, but his heart wasn't in the room.

So one week, the worship pastor, Angela, canceled practice and instead invited the team over for a time of shared devotion and prayer. They sang one song, unplugged, then read Psalm 51 together.

That night, something broke in Ethan. He confessed he had been dry spiritually, going through the motions. The team prayed over him. From that day forward, he became not just a player of chords but a carrier of God's presence.

Worship teams must become discipleship groups, not just music collectives. If you want worship that transforms the room, cultivate lives that are transformed offstage.

Create rhythms—weekly Scripture reflections, team check-ins, worship nights that are not for the congregation, but just for the team to be ministered to. Remember: the health of the platform is determined by the depth of the people on it.

In Exodus 33, we see that Moses worshiped in the tent of meeting, but Joshua lingered behind even after Moses left. That tells us something: those who dwell deeper will carry more of God's glory.

**Serving Others, Generosity, and Living Holy Lives**

Worship is not simply the vertical expression of song—it must overflow into horizontal expressions of love, holiness, and service.

Jesus made it very clear: the greatest commandments are to love the Lord your God, and to love your neighbor as yourself (Mark 12:30–31). The second is not an optional extra—it is the natural outflow of the first.

If we lift our hands in worship on Sunday but ignore the hurting, the poor, the broken, or the lonely during the week, we're living a disconnected gospel.

True worshipers are not just singers—they are servants. They feed the hungry. They forgive quickly. They give generously. They live in integrity when no one's watching. They show up for people who can't repay them. Their songs are matched by their surrender.

Let's remember Isaiah 1:13–17, where God, through the prophet, rejects the religious festivals and music of His people because their hearts and lives were corrupt. He says:

"Stop bringing meaningless offerings! ... Learn to do right; seek justice. Defend the oppressed."

It's a sobering reminder: God hears our lives louder than He hears our music.

Take the story of Lydia, a young worship leader in Mumbai. She was known for her powerful voice, but more so for her radical generosity. One day, when she learned that a family in their congregation couldn't afford school fees, she and her husband quietly paid the bill. They never told anyone. Months later, the family got saved and shared their testimony at a service—without even knowing who had helped them.

That, friends, is worship in action.

**Encouraging Worship in Homes, Small Groups, and Workplaces**

For worship to become a culture, it must leave the sanctuary and move into the spaces where life actually happens.

Worship in the home is where legacy is built. In Deuteronomy 6:6–7, God instructs the Israelites:

*"These commandments… are to be on your hearts. Impress them on your children. Talk about them when you sit at home and when you walk… tie them as symbols…"*

The home is the first church. The dinner table is an altar. Bedtime prayers are sacred.

Meet Reuben and Priya, parents of two kids, who decided that every Thursday night would be "Family Worship Night." They didn't have a guitar, so they played a worship playlist from YouTube, lit a candle, and read a Psalm. The kids would take turns praying. Their youngest, seven-year-old Ava, began asking if her friends could join.

Worship in the home is not just possible—it's powerful.

And what about small groups? These are often the most authentic environments for worship. Without the crowd or pressure, people sing louder, pray bolder, share deeper. Encourage worship leaders to attend and support small groups, even if they're not "leading." Sometimes, presence is more powerful than performance.

And yes—even the workplace is holy ground.

In Daniel 6, we see Daniel worshiping God three times a day in the midst of Babylon's government. He didn't need a mic—he had consistency.

Modern-day Daniels are all around us. Like Shalini, a corporate trainer who begins each workday with five minutes of worship in her car before stepping into the office. Her team says there's something about her peace that sets the tone. She says it's not her—it's Him.

Worship is not limited by geography. Wherever there is breath, there is an altar waiting to be built.

**Creating a Culture that Lives What It Sings**

In the end, we must ask ourselves:

*Are we creating a worship experience?*

*Or are we building a worshiping people?*

Because a culture of worship isn't measured by how loud the music is, but how deep the surrender is. It's seen in how people treat one another after the service. In how they serve, give, speak, and live.

The goal is not to be known as a "worshiping church" because of our sound. The goal is to be known as a worshiping people because of our substance.

A church where generosity flows like water.

A church where people forgive quickly and love deeply.

A church where Jesus is not just sung to, but seen in everyday actions.

That is the kind of worship God seeks.

As Jesus said in John 4:23–24:
*"Yet a time is coming and has now come when the true worshipers will worship the Father in spirit and in truth, for they are the kind of worshipers the Father seeks."*
Let us be that kind of church. Let us be those kinds of people.

**A Final Prayer: For Worship that Overflows**
*Father,*
*Make our worship more than music.*
*Make it our language. Our rhythm. Our heartbeat.*
*Teach us to glorify You with our lives—*
*in the way we serve, the way we love, the way we live.*
*Let our homes be filled with songs of gratitude.*
*Let our small groups become altars of intimacy.*
*Let our workplaces be touched by Your presence in us.*
*May we never be satisfied with stage worship alone.*
*May our lives preach louder than our lyrics.*
*In Jesus' name,*
*Amen.*

# Chapter 16: Evaluating and Adjusting the Worship Experience

There's something sacred about pausing long enough to look back—not with regret, but with reverence. To reflect not just on how well we played, but how deeply people met with Jesus. To ask, *"Did we just have a good set, or did we create space for a God-encounter?"*

In the book of Acts, the early church was constantly growing, shifting, and learning. Acts 2:42-47 shows a picture of a living, breathing body—devoted to teaching, breaking bread, prayer, and fellowship. And what followed was growth—both in numbers and in impact. That growth didn't come from complacency; it came from commitment to healthy rhythms and honest evaluation.

In the same way, our worship teams and experiences need space to pause, review, and recalibrate—not to fix what isn't broken, but to steward what is sacred. Evaluation, when done well, doesn't undermine passion—it refines it.

Let's explore what it looks like to evaluate worship experiences with humility, honesty, and hope, and how such a culture can lead to both depth and growth in your worship ministry.

**How to Do Honest, Healthy Evaluations**

Healthy evaluation isn't a performance review. It's not a checklist for flaws. It's a conversation that leads to growth. It asks: *Did we honor God? Did we serve people? Did we steward our gifts well?*

Too often, worship teams only debrief when something goes wrong. The mic fails, someone sings off-key, or the pastor runs over and the entire set gets cut. But the real power lies in building a rhythm of consistent, grace-filled evaluations, even when things go right.

Let me tell you about Cornerstone Chapel, a mid-sized church in Kochi. Their worship leader, Anil, began introducing ten-minute debriefs every Sunday right after the service. The rule was simple: "We speak truth in love, and we speak as a team, not at individuals."

One Sunday, the team had what felt like an electric worship experience—people were visibly moved, and the response was powerful. During the review, their drummer, Aaron, shared quietly, *"I played too busy in the last chorus—I felt the Spirit saying to wait, but I didn't."*

Nobody would have noticed. But it mattered to him. And the team learned something deeper: spiritual sensitivity matters more than technical excellence.

That's what evaluation does—it brings moments into focus, it sharpens the senses, it reminds us that God moments can be missed when we're in a hurry or distracted.

Now, let's be clear: evaluation should never become criticism dressed up in church clothes. If the purpose is to tear down, then we've missed the point entirely. Evaluation must be anchored in humility, encouragement, and shared vision.

Think of Jesus with His disciples. After sending them out, He gathered them again. In Luke 10, they returned excited about miracles, demons obeying, and authority. Jesus affirmed them—but also

reminded them: *"Don't rejoice that the spirits submit to you, but that your names are written in heaven."* Even in their victories, He redirected their focus. He evaluated their hearts, not just their results.
That's what we must aim for too—evaluation that draws people closer to Christ, not deeper into self-analysis.

**Listening to Feedback Without Losing Vision**

Feedback is a gift—but let's be honest, it doesn't always feel that way. Especially when it comes from unexpected places.
What do you do when Sister Prema says, *"The songs today weren't as spiritual as last week."* Or when a teenager says, *"Worship felt kinda boring."* Or when someone tells you the music was too loud, too soft, too slow, too modern, too traditional—all in one morning?
You listen. But you don't lose your vision.
Feedback is not always instruction. It is information. And wise leaders know the difference.
In Nehemiah 4, as the people rebuilt the walls of Jerusalem, opposition came from all sides. Critics tried to discourage them, twist their motives, and stall the work. But Nehemiah didn't abandon the mission. He listened when necessary. He guarded the work. But he stayed locked on the vision God had given him.
The same applies to worship leaders. Not every opinion is equal. But every voice matters. Listening doesn't mean reacting to every piece of feedback—it means filtering it through prayer, Scripture, and your team's core calling.
Meet Janice, a worship leader in Hyderabad. One Sunday, after introducing a new original song, a

longtime church member approached her and said, *"It's nice, but I miss the old hymns. They had more depth."*

At first, she felt deflated. But instead of brushing it off or overcorrecting, she invited the person to coffee. They talked, shared stories of faith, and by the end, Janice decided to include a short hymn medley once a month. The result? The congregation felt more connected. And her original songs were received with more openness.

She didn't lose the vision. She simply expanded the table.

**Monthly or Quarterly Worship Reviews with the Team**

One of the healthiest things a worship ministry can do is establish intentional rhythms of review. Weekly debriefs are great—but monthly or quarterly worship reviews allow for a broader, deeper conversation.

These sessions are not just about what happened—they're about where we're going.

At Riverflow Fellowship, a church in Bengaluru, every quarter the worship team gathers on a Saturday morning. They eat together, laugh, and then spend time going over:

- ✓ *What is working?*
- ✓ *What feels dry or routine?*
- ✓ *What songs have lost their impact?*
- ✓ *Who's feeling stretched? Who's feel sidelined?*
- ✓ *Are we following the Spirit—or just repeati formula?*

One quarter, they realized they hadn't written a song in nearly a year. Not because they couldn because they hadn't made space for it. So they aside a songwriting day. Out of it came a chorus that would eventually become their theme song for the year.

Another time, they recognized that their transitions between songs had become mechanical. So they began training team members to speak Scripture or short prayers during sets—not as a performance, but as a bridge into presence.

These reviews became refining moments—like pruning a healthy tree so it can bear more fruit.

**The Heart of It All**

Why does all this matter?

Because excellence in worship is not about impressing people—it's about stewarding encounters with God. It's about honoring the call, carrying the weight of spiritual leadership, and doing everything possible to create space for people to meet Jesus.

Evaluation, feedback, and review help us stay faithful to that call.

If worship is both art and offering, then we must care about how we shape it. Not to earn God's favor—but to honor the privilege of leading His people into His presence.

So take time. Reflect often. Ask questions. Seek the Spirit. Involve your team. Be open to change. And always—always—remember that the goal is not to get better at music. The goal is to get better at making room for God.

*Because in the end, the best worship services are not the ones where everything went perfectly…*

*They're the ones where Jesus was lifted high—and people were changed in His presence.*

# Chapter 17: Staying Spiritually Healthy as a Worship Leader

In the quiet moments before the lights turn on and the first chord is played, there's often a silent battle being fought in the heart of the worship leader. A battle between exhaustion and expectation. Between spiritual depth and the subtle drift toward performance. Between pouring out and running on empty.

No one sees this battle—not the congregation, not the band, not even the senior pastor sometimes. But it's real. And if left unaddressed, it can silently erode the very thing that drew us to worship ministry in the first place: a deep love for God and a desire to lead others into His presence.

This chapter is an honest look at that inner world. Because as worship leaders, we cannot lead people where we have not been ourselves. We can't give what we haven't received. If our soul is dry, our ministry will echo with emptiness, no matter how technically excellent we may sound.

Let's talk about staying spiritually healthy—not just for the sake of ministry, but for the sake of your soul.

**The Slow Fade of Burnout**

Burnout rarely announces its arrival with fanfare. It doesn't barge in loudly—it creeps in slowly.

It's the extra rehearsal you didn't have the strength for, but you showed up anyway. The late-night planning, the early morning service, the emails, the comparison, the weight of expectation. You tell yourself, *It's just a season*, but the season doesn't end.

I remember hearing the story of Ruth, a young worship leader at a growing church in Pune. Passionate, gifted, anointed. She was serving on three teams, leading worship for both youth and Sunday services, and also mentoring upcoming musicians. From the outside, it looked like she was thriving.

Until one Sunday, she didn't show up.

She wasn't sick. She wasn't rebellious. She was just... *empty*.

In her own words, "I didn't lose my love for Jesus. I just forgot to stop and sit with Him."

That struck a chord in me—and perhaps it does with you too. We get so busy with the act of worship that we sometimes neglect the heart of worship.

Even Elijah, one of the greatest prophets in the Old Testament, faced burnout. After calling down fire from heaven in 1 Kings 18, he finds himself in a cave in chapter 19, exhausted, fearful, and begging God to let him die. God's response? He doesn't rebuke Elijah. He feeds him. He lets him rest. And then He speaks—not through fire or earthquake, but a gentle whisper.

Burnout isn't weakness. It's a signal. And it often tells us what Elijah needed: Rest, nourishment, and renewal.

**Guarding Against Spiritual Dryness**

Spiritual dryness is more subtle than burnout. You might still be functioning—hitting every note, leading with power—but your heart feels distant. The Word doesn't stir you. Prayer becomes duty. Worship becomes a job, not a joy.

The Psalms give voice to this feeling. In Psalm 42, David cries out, *"Why are you cast down, O my soul? Why so disturbed within me?"* He's honest about the wilderness. He doesn't hide it. But he also speaks hope: *"Put your hope in God, for I will yet praise Him."*

Dryness isn't always sin-related. Sometimes, it's the byproduct of extended pouring without refilling. Sometimes it's grief. Or unprocessed disappointment. Or simply forgetting that your personal altar with God matters more than the stage.

Rajiv, a worship leader in Chennai, shared how spiritual dryness crept in after a season of back-to-back ministry. "I was still leading songs, but inside, I was disconnected. I couldn't remember the last time I worshipped when no one was watching."

That realization led him to take a three-week break—not from church, but from leading. He spent those weeks doing nothing but sitting with Scripture, walking in quiet, journaling, and worshipping alone in his room. "It wasn't magical," he said, "but I started hearing His voice again."

Sometimes, healing begins when we return to the secret place.

**The Importance of Personal Worship, Rest, and Renewal**

Let me say this as clearly as possible: Your personal worship life is more important than your public worship leadership. One fuels the other. One sustains the other.

Jesus modeled this rhythm. Even though He was constantly surrounded by crowds and ministry demands, He often withdrew to lonely places to pray

(Luke 5:16). He spent time with the Father before ministering to others.

If Jesus needed it, how much more do we?

Rest is not a luxury. It's a command. It's part of worship. Sabbath was God's idea—not because He needed a break, but because we do. It's how we remember that the ministry belongs to Him, not us.

Take time to unplug. Worship when no one is looking. Go for a walk. Watch a sunrise. Play a song not because you have to, but because your heart is stirred.

One of the most powerful things I ever heard a worship pastor say was this: *"My goal isn't just to lead others in worship. It's to be a worshipper when no one's in the room."*

When that becomes your posture, you'll find your soul refilling—not instantly, but faithfully.

**Having Mentors and Spiritual Covering**

There's a dangerous lie that leaders often believe: *I have to be strong for everyone else.*

But the truth is, even leaders need shepherds. Even worship leaders need to be led.

Mentorship isn't about control—it's about covering. About having people in your life who can ask the hard questions, pray over you, and remind you of who you are when you forget.

Paul mentored Timothy, reminding him to fan into flame the gift of God within him (2 Timothy 1:6). Elijah mentored Elisha. Moses mentored Joshua. Leadership in the Bible was rarely done in isolation.

Let me introduce you to Shanthi, a veteran worship leader in Delhi. She's been leading for over 25 years. When younger leaders ask her the secret to longevity, she says, *"It's not my voice. It's not my discipline. It's the people who've prayed for me when I had nothing left."*

She meets monthly with her spiritual mentor—a retired missionary who listens, speaks life, and reminds her that she is first a daughter of God, not a performer for God.

You need that too. Whether it's a pastor, a counselor, or a wise elder—someone who can see past your title and into your soul.

Don't wait until crisis hits. Pursue covering now.

**Finishing Well**

In the end, staying spiritually healthy isn't about surviving ministry—it's about finishing well. About being able to say, like Paul in 2 Timothy 4:7, *"I have fought the good fight, I have finished the race, I have kept the faith."*

No song, no stage, no spotlight is worth sacrificing your soul.

Your calling is too precious. Your intimacy with Jesus is too valuable. And the people you lead deserve a leader who is not just gifted—but grounded. Not just anointed—but abiding.

So take care of your soul.

Worship with tears when needed. Rest without guilt. Speak truth to those around you. Find safe spaces. Let God lead you before you lead anyone else.

*Because when the heart of the worship leader is healthy, the whole house begins to sing.*

# Chapter 18: Navigating Conflict and Disunity

Conflict. Just the word can make even the strongest worship leader want to shrink back. And yet, wherever there are people, there will be friction. And wherever there is friction, there is opportunity—for division or for growth.

If you've served on a worship team for any length of time, you've probably experienced it: a team member offended by a scheduling change, a disagreement about the musical direction of a song, or unspoken tension between musicians that silently simmers during rehearsals. Sometimes the elephant in the room plays louder than the instruments.

Let's face it: worship ministry, while sacred, is still ministry among humans. We're not immune to emotion, ego, or exhaustion. But here's the good news—conflict doesn't have to be a death sentence for a team. In fact, when handled well, it can lead to deeper trust, stronger unity, and clearer communication.

This chapter is about how we deal with tension biblically, humbly, and wisely, so we can guard the sacred atmosphere of worship ministry.

## When Heaven Meets Humanity: The Inevitable Collision

Worship is a divine assignment carried out through human vessels. That's both beautiful and messy. Sometimes we wrongly assume that because we're doing "spiritual work," conflict shouldn't exist. But the early church, filled with the Holy Spirit and led by apostles, faced conflict too.

In Acts 6, there was a dispute between the Hellenistic Jews and the Hebraic Jews over food distribution. That may seem like a mundane issue, but it had the potential to divide the early believers. The apostles didn't ignore the problem. They listened, delegated, and empowered, resolving the tension with wisdom and fairness.

In another powerful example, Paul and Barnabas—two spiritual giants and partners in ministry—had a "sharp disagreement" (Acts 15:39) about whether to take John Mark with them on their next mission. The disagreement was so intense that they parted ways.

Was it ideal? No. But even in the fracture, the Kingdom expanded—Paul took Silas, Barnabas took Mark, and both teams continued ministry. And later, Paul would even commend Mark again (2 Timothy 4:11), showing us that reconciliation and restoration are always possible.

**Team Tensions: Real Worship Team Stories**

Let me introduce you to a few friends—composites of many real stories from worship leaders I've mentored.

Neha was the lead vocalist at a thriving church in Mumbai. Talented, humble, and deeply spiritual. But she felt consistently overlooked by the worship leader, Daniel, who often favored a newer vocalist for solo moments. Neha didn't speak up, but bitterness began to creep in. Rehearsals became tense. Eye contact was avoided. Eventually, it started to affect the atmosphere on stage.

On the other hand, Daniel felt pressured to spotlight the new vocalist because she connected well with the congregation. He had no idea Neha was hurting.

Miscommunication grew roots, and unity was slowly being choked.

The breakthrough came not through a structured meeting but through intentional vulnerability. Neha finally shared her heart—not in accusation, but in honesty. Daniel listened. They both wept. Daniel admitted his oversight, and Neha repented for harboring resentment.

From that day on, something shifted. Their worship deepened—not just musically, but relationally. And the congregation felt it.

This is what happens when we confront conflict with humility rather than avoid it out of fear.

**Biblical Steps to Reconciliation**

Jesus Himself gave us a blueprint for dealing with conflict within the body of Christ. In Matthew 18:15–17, He outlines a three-step process:

1. Go to the person privately. If someone offends you, your first step isn't to post about it, complain to others, or silently withdraw—it's to go to them directly and privately. Jesus values relationship enough to encourage conversation over gossip.
2. Bring witnesses if needed. If the first conversation doesn't bring clarity or peace, bring along one or two spiritually mature believers who can help mediate. This isn't about ganging up—it's about creating a safe space for reconciliation.
3. Involve leadership only when necessary. If the issue still can't be resolved, then and only then, Jesus says to involve church leadership. The goal at every stage is restoration, not punishment.

But beyond process, reconciliation is about posture—the posture of the heart.

Paul writes in Colossians 3:13: *"Bear with each other and forgive one another…Forgive as the Lord forgave you."* That's the standard. Not what they deserve, not how bad the offense was, but how Christ forgave us.

**Protecting Unity as a Sacred Priority**

Unity isn't a side goal of worship ministry—it is the very foundation upon which worship stands.

In Psalm 133, we read: *"How good and pleasant it is when brothers live together in unity…for there the Lord commands the blessing."* Unity invites blessing. Disunity, even hidden beneath the surface, blocks it.

Jesus prayed in John 17—His final hours before the cross—that His followers would be one, even as He and the Father are one. He didn't pray for bigger crowds, better sound systems, or flawless vocals. He prayed for oneness.

Why? Because unity reflects the heart of God.

As worship leaders, our job is not only to create music but to protect the spiritual climate of our teams. That means calling out gossip, gently correcting divisive behavior, and creating a culture where feedback is safe and humility is honored.

I know a worship pastor, Manoj, who begins every team retreat with one powerful question: *"Is there anyone here we need to reconcile with before we go any further?"* Sometimes, the team ends up spending the first hour hugging, crying, and praying together before a single chord is played.

What flows out of that space? Power. Presence. Purity of worship.

### Creating a Culture of Peace and Open Communication

You don't have to wait for conflict to arise to begin cultivating unity. It begins with proactive conversations, honest check-ins, and a shared language of grace.

Ask your team members often: *"How are you doing—not just musically, but spiritually? Emotionally?"*

Create safe rhythms for debriefing after services, where the focus is not just on performance, but relational health.

Teach your team that feedback is not a threat—it's a gift. That hard conversations are not something to fear—they're part of growing in Christlikeness.

Let every worship team member know: *You are not just here for your instrument. You're here for your heart. For your relationships. For the unity of this house.*

### When Unity Is Tested—And Triumphs

Disunity doesn't disqualify a team from worship—it reminds us that we are still being sanctified, still growing. What disqualifies us is ignoring it.

Unity is tested most in seasons of pressure—during transitions, during spiritual battles, or when personalities clash. But these are the moments when God gives us a choice: to either give in to offense or to grow in love.

I've seen teams who once fractured become stronger than ever because they chose humility over pride, grace over judgment, and restoration over resentment.

And that's the kind of team God blesses.

### In Closing

Conflict is not the enemy. Disunity is. Conflict, when handled with Christlike love and biblical wisdom, becomes a tool for growth.

So as worship leaders, let's commit to protecting the sacred space of unity—not just on the platform, but in the greenroom, the group chat, and the heart.

Let's speak truth in love. Let's pursue one another with the same grace Jesus has shown us. Let's be peacemakers—not peacekeepers, not avoiders, but builders of true reconciliation.

*Because when the body is united, the sound of worship rises—not just in harmony, but in heavenly agreement.*

# Chapter 19: Revival-Focused Worship Leadership

There is something deep and stirring about a heart that burns not just to lead worship, but to host revival. True revival doesn't come merely from increased activity, clever programming, or emotional hype—it comes when the presence of God invades hearts in such a way that transformation becomes inevitable. Worship leaders, when called by God, are not just song leaders or music directors—they become fire carriers, altar keepers, and forerunners of God's movement in a generation.

**Praying for Breakthrough in Worship Services**

Before revival is seen publicly, it is often felt privately in prayer. There is no shortcut to revival that bypasses the secret place. Every worship leader who desires to see heaven touch earth during a service must learn to become familiar with the presence of God off the stage. It is here that the seeds of revival are watered.

Miriam, a worship leader at a small church in Tamil Nadu, often found herself frustrated that the congregation didn't seem moved during worship. The songs were solid, the musicians were skilled, yet there was a sense of dryness. After seeking counsel from her mentor, she began committing every Saturday night to prayer—not just to go through the songs again, but to ask for a fresh revelation of Jesus, to repent for any pride or distraction, and to intercede for those who would attend. Over time, something changed. The room remained the same, the setlist wasn't radically different, but people began to weep during songs, kneel unprompted, and testify of healings and breakthroughs.

That's the hidden power of prayer—it tills the ground of people's hearts before they arrive, allowing the Spirit to move freely. In Acts 4:31, we see the early church pray, and "the place where they were meeting was shaken." Worship leaders must believe again in a God who shakes places—and be willing to ask for it.

**Discernment and Prophetic Leading in Worship**

Revival worship doesn't follow a rigid script; it flows with the Spirit. Discernment is a gift that is cultivated through intimacy with God. It's about sensing when to stay in a moment, when to move on, when to repeat a chorus, or when to pause entirely in silence.

Elisha, in 2 Kings 3, asked for a musician to play before he gave a prophetic word. It was as the music began that "the hand of the Lord came upon him" (2 Kings 3:15). This moment highlights the profound relationship between worship and the prophetic. Sometimes, a simple melody becomes the backdrop for God to speak.

In a modern-day example, Jacob, a worship leader in a bustling city church, shared how during one Sunday service, while leading a popular song, he suddenly felt a deep weight in his spirit and an impression to stop. Against all human logic, he brought the music to a hush and simply said, "There's someone here who feels forgotten, and God wants you to know He sees you." A woman in the third row burst into tears—she had told the Lord that very morning, "If You see me, have someone say it."

This wasn't about showmanship—it was a moment of divine appointment, and it came because the leader was listening.

Discernment means being willing to surrender the plan for the presence. It is risky. It is vulnerable. But it is how revival moments are born.

**Fasting, Intercession, and Preparing the Altar**

There is an invisible altar every worship leader builds before Sunday ever arrives. It is not made of wood or stone—it is made of sacrifice, surrender, and fire from heaven. Fasting and intercession become tools to prepare this altar.

Joel 2:12-13 calls the people of Israel to return to the Lord "with all your heart, with fasting and weeping and mourning." This call to consecration always precedes the outpouring. In Joel 2:28, after this return, God declares, "I will pour out my Spirit on all people." Revival is not a random event; it is a response to radical surrender.

In the church where Lydia led worship, the team began practicing monthly fasts. They would fast together—not just from food, but from distractions. On these days, they prayed for each other, for the congregation, and specifically for people far from God. Slowly, their worship culture shifted. People who were once passive began to raise their hands, sing louder, and show up earlier. Visitors commented on a "tangible peace" in the room. No marketing campaign did this. It was the power of a people who prepared the altar.

Fasting strips us of dependency on flesh. Intercession makes room for heaven's agenda. And preparing the altar—through spiritual discipline, integrity, and unity—invites the fire of God to fall.

**Revival is the Fruit of Reverence and Risk**

Every worship leader must ask themselves: Are we playing it safe, or are we preparing for a move of God? Revival doesn't happen on accident. It is the result of a people willing to contend, to yield, and to believe that God wants to do more than we've seen.

One cannot speak of revival worship without remembering the example of King David. In 2 Samuel 6, David brings the ark of God back to Jerusalem. His worship is so extravagant—dancing before the Lord with all his might—that his wife Michal despises him for it. But David understood something: revival worship doesn't aim to impress—it exists to honor the presence of the King.

David prepared a tabernacle, not just with songs but with structure—24/7 worship, multiple musicians, and a priority of presence. This model, the Tabernacle of David, is often referenced in discussions on worship and revival because it placed God's presence at the center of national life. That is what we are called to restore—not a copy of the past, but the heart of a people radically aligned to the worthiness of God.

Revival-focused worship leadership is not a technique—it is a posture. It's the fire behind the music, the hunger behind the plan, the humility behind the mic. It is a holy invitation to co-labor with God in leading a generation into deep encounter. Worship leaders who burn for revival will not settle for performance. They will press in, pray through, and prepare the altar until His glory comes.

And when it does, everything changes.

# Conclusion: Worship Leadership as Kingdom Stewardship

When all the songs have faded and the lights have dimmed, when the stage is empty and the sound system is silent, what remains is the heart of the worship leader—the heart of a steward. Worship leadership is not simply about planning a perfect Sunday or leading a flawless set. It is about stewarding something sacred, something ancient, something that touches eternity: the worship of the Living God.

This calling is not casual. It is not a career path or a stage opportunity. It is holy.

**Your Calling is Holy**

God has never treated worship as entertainment, and neither should we. From the very beginning, He established worship as a space of divine meeting, a sacred act that required reverence, purity, and intentionality. When Moses stood before the burning bush, God said, "Take off your sandals, for the place where you are standing is holy ground" (Exodus 3:5). Holiness wasn't in the soil—it was in the presence. That same presence now dwells within us, and as worship leaders, we are entrusted with creating atmospheres where others can encounter it.

Elias, a worship leader from a rural village in Kenya, understood this well. He had no fancy equipment, no band, not even electricity most weeks. But he had a deep sense of God's holiness. Every time he led worship under the open skies, he would fast the day before, not out of legalism, but out of awe. He believed that leading people before the throne of the King required preparation—not just musical, but spiritual. And because of this posture, God moved powerfully among the people. Healing, repentance, and salvation flowed regularly, even without microphones or LED screens.

Worship leading is more than skill; it is a sacred trust. When we forget that, we risk turning ministry into performance and calling into career.

**Worship Leaders as Modern-Day Levites**

In the Old Testament, the tribe of Levi was set apart for the service of the tabernacle and the temple. They didn't receive land like the other tribes—their inheritance was the Lord Himself (Deuteronomy 10:9). Among the Levites were the sons of Asaph, Heman, and Jeduthun—musicians and singers appointed by David for the ministry of worship (1 Chronicles 25).

These were not part-time volunteers or casual singers. They were full-time ministers before the presence of God. They stood daily, offering thanksgiving and praise, maintaining the rhythms of worship that kept the fire on the altar burning.

In many ways, today's worship leaders are the modern-day Levites. No longer confined to a temple made of stone, we now minister before God in Spirit and truth (John 4:23). Our platform is not a stage—it's the presence. Our instrument is not just a guitar or keyboard—it's our life. Like the Levites, we are called to serve with purity, consistency, and faithfulness, regardless of applause or recognition.

Sophia, a young worship leader in Singapore, once told her team, "If we only worship passionately when we are on stage, we are not Levites—we are actors." Her words stung, but they were true. True Levites worship in the secret place before they ever step into the public space. They carry the ark, even when it's heavy, and they don't let the fire go out.

**Leaving a Legacy of Worship That's Not About Us—but All About Him**

One day, your name will be forgotten. The songs you wrote may fade. The videos may be archived. But what you build in the spirit, what you leave in the hearts of people, that remains.

Worship leadership is not about building a platform for ourselves—it's about building an altar for Him. It's not about gathering followers, but about leading followers to Jesus. When John the Baptist said, "He must increase, but I must decrease" (John 3:30), he wasn't displaying insecurity—he was modeling the true heart of a Kingdom steward.

Every act of selfless worship, every moment of Spirit-led leadership, every time you point people to Jesus instead of yourself—you are writing a legacy. Not in the history books of men, but in the heart of the Church and the records of heaven.

Paul, in his final letter to Timothy, said, "I have fought the good fight, I have finished the race, I have kept the faith" (2 Timothy 4:7). That's the cry of a true worship leader—not "I sang the most solos," or "I had the best voice," but "I stayed faithful to my calling. I led them to Jesus."

Let me tell you about Jordan, a worship leader who served quietly in a small-town church in Pennsylvania for over 35 years. He wasn't famous, didn't write songs for radio, and never traveled. But he taught generations how to worship. He discipled his team, raised up leaders, and consistently pointed people to Jesus. When he passed away, hundreds showed up to his memorial, not because he was a celebrity—but because he had led them into the presence of God over and over again. His legacy wasn't his name. It was His name—Jesus.

Worship leaders, your stewardship matters. Heaven is watching. The next generation is watching.

*What kind of worship legacy will you leave behind?*

*Will it be one built on personal ambition or eternal impact?*

*Will it be filled with noise or with presence?*

*Will it point to your greatness or to His glory?*

This calling—this holy calling—is not just about Sundays. It's about eternity. May we be found faithful, not famous. And may every song, every service, every sacrifice lead the Church to the One who alone is worthy.

Jesus at the center. Always.

Forever.

Let this final chapter serve not as a conclusion but as a commissioning—for every worship leader who dares to dream beyond the setlist, who dares to lead not for applause but for awakening, and who dares to live and lead for the glory of the King.

# Appendices

# Appendix A: Weekly Devotional Plan for Worship Teams

***Strengthening the Spirit Behind the Sound***

**Week 1: The Heart Before the Sound**

**Scripture:** *1 Samuel 16:7* – "Man looks at the outward appearance, but the Lord looks at the heart."

**Reflection:**

Before you ever pick up a mic or step behind a keyboard, God has already tuned in—not to your melody, but to your motives. Saul had the stature of a king, but David had the heart of a worshiper. God is still searching for worshipers who care more about pleasing Him in private than impressing people in public. Worship begins in the unseen places of humility, reverence, and surrender.

**Challenge:**

Ask God to search your heart this week. Is there any pride, comparison, or bitterness you're carrying into rehearsals or the platform? Lay it down. Begin afresh.

---

**Week 2: Serving with One Spirit**

**Scripture:** *Philippians 2:2* – "Make my joy complete by being like-minded, having the same love, being one in spirit and of one mind."

**Reflection:**

A worship team is not a collection of soloists—it is a family. Unity is not the absence of conflict but the presence of mutual honor. When we serve one another with love and humility, the presence of God rests on our collective offering. Harmony offstage creates anointing onstage.

**Challenge:**

This week, encourage one teammate intentionally. Pray for them, serve them, bless them—without expecting anything in return.

---

**Week 3: Worship Is War**

**Scripture:** *2 Chronicles 20:21* – "Jehoshaphat appointed singers to walk ahead of the army, singing to the Lord..."

**Reflection:**

Worship is not soft; it's strategic. In the spirit realm, it disarms fear, breaks chains, and invites God to move. Jehoshaphat didn't send swords first—he sent singers. When you stand to lead, you are not performing; you are contending for the hearts of people and the presence of God to come.

**Challenge:**

Identify a stronghold—fear, heaviness, division—and declare worship over it this week. Begin rehearsals with warfare worship.

---

**Week 4: Leading People to Jesus, Not to Us**

**Scripture:** *John 12:32* – "And I, when I am lifted up from the earth, will draw all people to Myself."

**Reflection:**

Charisma can draw a crowd. Only Christ can change hearts. As worship leaders, we are not the destination—we are the signpost pointing to Him. Our joy is not in being seen, but in seeing Him glorified. We must decrease, so He may increase.

**Challenge:**

Before leading worship this week, pray: "Jesus, let

them see You, not me." Mean it. Watch what happens.

---

**Week 5: Clean Hands and Pure Hearts**
**Scripture:** *Psalm 24:3-4* – "Who may ascend the mountain of the Lord? He who has clean hands and a pure heart…"
**Reflection:**
God doesn't need perfect people, but He does desire purity. Worship that pleases Him flows from a life that seeks holiness. The platform is not a place to hide compromise—it is a place to reflect His holiness. Don't let talent outpace integrity.
**Challenge:**
This week, confess one area of struggle to God—and to a trusted mentor or leader. Pursue purity. It's worth it.

---

**Week 6: A Lifestyle, Not a Setlist**
**Scripture:** *Romans 12:1* – "Offer your bodies as a living sacrifice, holy and pleasing to God—this is your true and proper worship."
**Reflection:**
What you do in your living room matters more than what you do on the stage. Worship is not an event; it is a life laid down. A surrendered lifestyle sings louder than a Sunday song.
**Challenge:**
Worship God this week through a non-musical act: serve someone, give generously, forgive freely. Let your life sing.

---

**Week 7: Restoring Joy in Worship**
**Scripture:** *Psalm 51:12* – "Restore to me the joy of your salvation and grant me a willing spirit, to sustain me."
**Reflection:**
It's easy for worship leading to become routine—another rehearsal, another set, another Sunday. But God never intended worship to be mechanical. He created it to be an overflow of joy, of awe, of wonder. If you've lost your fire, He's not angry—He's inviting you back to His presence.
**Challenge:**
Take one night this week and worship alone, not to prepare, but to be refreshed. Sing a new song. Dance if you want. Just enjoy Him.

---

**Week 8: Finishing Strong**
**Scripture:** *2 Timothy 4:7* – "I have fought the good fight, I have finished the race, I have kept the faith."
**Reflection:**
Consistency in worship leadership is rare, but it is deeply powerful. Some will sing louder, others play better—but those who finish faithful will wear the crown. God is not impressed with one-time flames; He's looking for those who burn with steady devotion.
**Challenge:**
Reflect on your journey. Where has God brought you from? Where are you headed? Recommit to finishing strong—not for the stage, but for the Savior.

---

**Week 9: God's Presence Over Perfection**
**Scripture:** *Exodus 33:15* – "Then Moses said to Him, 'If Your Presence does not go with us, do not send us up from here.'"

**Reflection:**
Moses understood something powerful: perfection in performance is useless without the presence of God. You can have flawless harmonies and breathtaking transitions, but if His presence is missing, it's just noise. God's presence is the *only* thing that transforms lives in worship.
**Challenge:**
This week, ask God to increase your hunger for His presence above your desire for performance. Lay down the need to impress and lean into intimacy with Him.

---

**Week 10: Hidden Before Honored**
**Scripture:** *Luke 2:52* – "And Jesus grew in wisdom and stature, and in favor with God and man."
**Reflection:**
Even Jesus went through years of growth and preparation before stepping into public ministry. In worship, many long for platforms before they've embraced preparation. Growth in the hidden place determines fruitfulness in the open place. Let God do a deep work in secret.
**Challenge:**
Dedicate intentional time this week to your private walk with God—reading, journaling, and listening. Let Him mold you in the quiet.

---

**Week 11: Spirit Over Structure**
**Scripture:** *Galatians 5:25* – "Since we live by the Spirit, let us keep in step with the Spirit."
**Reflection:**
Setlists matter. Soundchecks are helpful. But if we're not listening to the Holy Spirit, we risk leading a service He's not in. The Spirit often moves beyond

our plans—prompting a spontaneous song, a moment of silence, or an unexpected breakthrough. Be structured, but stay sensitive.

**Challenge:**

In rehearsal this week, pause to ask the Holy Spirit if He has something different in mind. Leave room for Him to redirect.

---

**Week 12: Excellence Reflects God's Nature**

**Scripture:** *Colossians 3:23* – "Whatever you do, work at it with all your heart, as working for the Lord."

**Reflection:**

Excellence in worship is not about ego—it's about reflecting the beauty and order of our God. He is not sloppy or careless; His works are wondrous. When we strive for excellence, not perfectionism, we give Him our best because He gave us His.

**Challenge:**

This week, find one small area in your worship preparation to improve—musicianship, punctuality, planning, communication—and offer it to God as worship.

---

**Week 13: The Power of the First Note**

**Scripture**: *2 Kings 3:15* – "But now bring me a harpist. While the harpist was playing, the hand of the Lord came upon Elisha."

**Reflection:**

There is a moment in worship where something shifts—a sound that opens the heavens, like Elisha experienced with the harpist. Never underestimate the power of the first note. It's not filler; it's a doorway for the Spirit to move. Come ready. Come expectant.

**Challenge:**

Pray before the *first* note this week. Ask God to move

from the moment the music begins and to make your sound a signal to heaven.

---

**Week 14: Leading with Brokenness**
**Scripture:** *Psalm 51:17* – "The sacrifices of God are a broken spirit; a broken and contrite heart, O God, You will not despise."
**Reflection:**
You don't need to have it all together to lead. In fact, your vulnerability may be the very thing that brings others to Jesus. Brokenness isn't weakness—it's an offering. Bring your real self before God. He uses cracked vessels to pour out His Spirit.
**Challenge:**
This week, share a testimony or struggle in your next team devotion or group chat. Let others see how God meets you in your mess.

---

**Week 15: Staying Soft in the Spirit**
**Scripture:** *Hebrews 3:15* – "Today, if you hear His voice, do not harden your hearts…"
**Reflection:**
Over time, disappointment, offense, or routine can harden even the most sincere worshiper's heart. But sensitivity to God requires softness—a heart willing to be moved again. Don't allow leadership or ministry to desensitize you. Stay tender.
**Challenge:**
Invite the Lord to show you any places where your heart has become calloused. Ask Him to soften you again. Weep if needed. Let it go.

---

**Week 16: Beyond the Platform—A Servant's Heart**
**Scripture:** *Mark 10:45* – "For even the Son of Man did not come to be served, but to serve…"
**Reflection:**
Jesus didn't demand a spotlight. He washed feet. Worship leaders are not performers—they are servants. Help carry cables. Pray with the ushers. Greet people in the lobby. The greatest worship happens offstage when no one is watching.
**Challenge:**
Do a behind-the-scenes act of service this week that no one expects—and don't tell anyone about it. Let it be between you and God.

---

**Week 17: When God Says Wait**
**Scripture:** *Habakkuk 2:3* – "Though it linger, wait for it; it will certainly come and will not delay."
**Reflection:**
Every worshiper will walk through a "waiting season"—waiting for breakthrough, a word, or revival. But the waiting isn't wasted. It shapes us. Trust is refined in the delay. Keep showing up. Keep singing. The rain will come.
**Challenge:**
Identify one promise or dream you're still waiting on. Offer it to God this week, and choose to worship in the waiting.

---

**Week 18: Worship Is Your Weapon**
**Scripture:** *Acts 16:25-26* – "About midnight Paul and Silas were praying and singing hymns to God… and suddenly there was a violent earthquake…"
**Reflection:**
Worship doesn't just respond to freedom—it releases

it. Paul and Silas didn't wait for deliverance before they praised; their praise *brought* the breakthrough. In worship, shackles fall, not just for you, but for everyone listening.

**Challenge:**

This week, worship like you believe prison doors can open. Lead with boldness. Declare freedom over your team and church.

---

**Week 19: An Audience of One**

**Scripture:** *Matthew 6:6* – "But when you pray, go into your room, close the door and pray to your Father, who is unseen. Then your Father, who sees what is done in secret, will reward you."

**Reflection:**

Worship isn't a show. It's not for the congregation. It's not for your worship leader. It's for One—the King of Kings. The moment our hearts shift from pleasing people to honoring God, our worship becomes holy. True worship leaders carry a hidden life before the Lord long before they lead publicly.

**Challenge:**

This week, worship in private like no one is watching—because only He truly matters. Sing in your car. Dance in your room. Minister to the Lord alone.

---

**Week 20: The Joy of the Lord Is Your Strength**

**Scripture:** *Nehemiah 8:10* – "...Do not grieve, for the joy of the Lord is your strength."

**Reflection:**

Ministry can be draining, and sometimes joy feels like a luxury. But joy is not just a feeling—it's a source of strength. Joy in the Lord strengthens your voice, your stamina, your spirit, and your presence on the platform. Joy is a weapon against burnout and heaviness.

**Challenge:**

Ask God to restore joy in your worship this week. Smile when you sing. Dance lightly in rehearsal. Choose joy intentionally and watch strength return.

---

**Week 21: Carrying the Ark Reverently**

**Scripture:** *2 Samuel 6:6-7* – "When they came to the threshing floor of Nakon, Uzzah reached out and took hold of the ark… The Lord's anger burned against Uzzah…"

**Reflection:**

The Ark of the Covenant symbolized God's presence. When Uzzah handled it casually, it cost him his life. As worship leaders, we too carry God's presence—and we must do so with reverence. Familiarity must never lead to flippancy. We are stewards of something holy.

**Challenge:**

Before you step into rehearsal or a service this week, pause and acknowledge the holiness of your role. Handle His presence with awe.

---

**Week 22: Tuning More Than Instruments**

**Scripture:** *Psalm 139:23-24* – "Search me, God, and know my heart… See if there is any offensive way in me."

**Reflection:**

We spend time tuning our guitars, syncing our tracks, and rehearsing transitions. But what about our hearts? Are they in tune with God's heart? A bitter spirit or prideful attitude can derail worship faster than a wrong chord. Inner tuning is just as important as outer preparation.

**Challenge:**
Invite God to examine your heart this week. Ask a trusted teammate for feedback. Confess any attitude that needs realignment before the Lord.

---

**Week 23: The Anointing Makes the Difference**
**Scripture:** *Isaiah 10:27* – "...the yoke shall be destroyed because of the anointing."
**Reflection:**
Skill may impress people, but only the anointing breaks yokes. Anointed worship lifts burdens and ignites faith. The anointing is not earned—it's cultivated through prayer, obedience, and closeness with God. Chase Him, not fame. Seek His touch, not applause.
**Challenge:**
Set aside one day this week to fast or pray specifically for greater anointing. Ask the Holy Spirit to rest on you afresh when you lead.

---

**Week 24: Don't Miss the Moment**
**Scripture:** *Luke 19:44* – "...because you did not recognize the time of God's coming to you."
**Reflection:**
Sometimes we're so focused on executing the setlist that we miss the moment when heaven wants to break in. Worship leaders are called to *discern* what God is doing—not just deliver what's planned. Don't miss the moment. Be interruptible. Be watchful.
**Challenge:**
In your next set, watch for divine moments—unexpected stillness, spontaneous songs, or tears in the room. Partner with God in those moments.

---

**Week 25: The Oil Comes from the Pressing**
**Scripture**: *2 Corinthians 4:8-9* – "We are hard pressed on every side, but not crushed…"
**Reflection:**
Olive oil—symbolic of the Holy Spirit—comes only from pressing. Likewise, your most anointed worship will often flow from seasons of struggle. God doesn't waste your pain. He uses it to produce oil. The fragrance that rises from brokenness touches hearts in a way nothing else can.
**Challenge:**
If you're in a difficult season, don't run from the pressing. Embrace it. Let God produce oil that heals others through your worship.

---

**Week 26: Building Altars, Not Stages**
**Scripture:** *Genesis 12:7* – "So Abram built an altar there to the Lord, who had appeared to him."
**Reflection:**
Altars are places of sacrifice. Stages are places of performance. God calls us to build altars—places where He meets us, where we surrender and He descends. Every time we lead worship, we're not just singing—we're building a space for God to meet His people.
**Challenge:**
This week, before you lead, ask yourself: am I building an altar or just walking onto a stage? Bring Him a sacrifice.

---

**Week 27: A United Sound**
**Scripture:** *Acts 2:1* – "When the day of Pentecost came, they were all together in one place."
**Reflection:**
There is supernatural power in unity. At Pentecost,

the Spirit came *when* the people were one. Disunity on a worship team blocks the flow of the Spirit. But when hearts align in humility, prayer, and love—heaven opens. One sound. One purpose. One voice.

**Challenge:**

Meet with a teammate this week to pray together or share a meal. Strengthen your bond. Worship is warfare—and unity is your shield.

---

**Week 28: Obedience Over Opportunity**

**Scripture:** *1 Samuel 15:22* – "To obey is better than sacrifice…"

**Reflection:**

We often crave opportunities—bigger platforms, more influence—but God values obedience more. The most anointed worshipers are those who say "yes" in the unseen places: to serve, to wait, to let go. Obedience is what God rewards, not visibility.

**Challenge:**

Ask God if there's an area of obedience He's waiting on from you. Then do it—joyfully and quietly, knowing it pleases Him.

---

**Week 29: Rest Is an Act of Trust**

**Scripture:** *Psalm 127:2* – "...He gives sleep to His beloved."

**Reflection:**

Sometimes, in the name of ministry, we overextend ourselves. But rest is not laziness—it's trust. It says, "God, I don't have to strive because You sustain it." True rest is not just physical, but spiritual. It resets your soul and reminds you who's really in control.

**Challenge:**

Schedule real rest this week—no rehearsals, no

setlists, no screens. Be still. Let your soul breathe in His presence.

---

**Week 30: Finish with Faithfulness**
**Scripture:** *2 Timothy 4:7* – "I have fought the good fight, I have finished the race, I have kept the faith."
**Reflection:**
God is not looking for flashy. He's looking for faithful. Some seasons will be thrilling, others mundane. But finishing well matters more than starting strong. A worshiper who stays consistent, humble, and anchored in Christ will leave an eternal legacy.
**Challenge:**
Reflect on your worship journey. Where has God brought you? Where is He taking you? Commit again to finish your race in faithfulness.

---

# Continuing the Journey: Creating Your Own Devotionals as a Worship Team

Your team has just walked through 30 weeks of being shaped, strengthened, and stirred through weekly devotionals. But this is not the end—it's only the beginning. As a worship leader or team member, you are now invited to take ownership of your team's spiritual journey by creating devotionals of your own. Here's a simple and spirit-led path to help you do just that.

**1. Start with the Secret Place**
Before you even write a word, spend time with God. Listen. Read the Word slowly. Let the Holy Spirit

highlight a verse, a phrase, or a moment that resonates with where your team is. Often, the most powerful devotionals are birthed out of personal encounter.

Ask:

- ✓ What is the Lord speaking to *me* right now?
- ✓ What does my team need to hear this week?

**2. Choose a Core Scripture**

Every devotional begins with God's Word. Choose one Scripture that captures the heart of what God is saying. This could come from your own quiet time or be inspired by the season your team is in—joy, warfare, transition, burnout, breakthrough, etc.

Examples:

- ✓ Times of waiting: *Isaiah 40:31*
- ✓ Tiredness or burnout: *Matthew 11:28–30*
- ✓ Desiring deeper intimacy: *Psalm 27:4*

**3. Reflect Deeply, Not Theologically**

You don't need to be a Bible scholar. Write from your heart. Keep it real, honest, and practical. Think of your devotional as a conversation with your team—not a sermon. Draw from your own life, struggles, or recent breakthroughs.

Ask:

- ✓ Why does this verse matter right now?
- ✓ How can I connect this truth to worship?
- ✓ Is there a personal story or team moment that illustrates it?

**4. Apply It to Worship Leadership**

Always bridge the truth to what you do as a worshiper and leader. Help your team see how Scripture shapes their heart, their posture, their

preparation, and their platform. This is what transforms a Bible verse into a worship lifestyle.
Example:
If you reflect on *John 15:5 (Abide in Me)*, you might remind your team that fruitfulness in worship comes not from effort but from remaining connected to the Vine—even during rehearsals, transitions, and technical glitches.

**5. Add a Challenge or Response**
End your devotional with one practical challenge or question. Invite your team to do something about what they've read—pray, repent, sing, reflect, reach out, or simply pause.
Keep it simple:
- ✓ "This week, find 10 minutes to worship with no agenda."
- ✓ "Ask God what it means to surrender again."
- ✓ "Encourage one teammate before the next set."

**6. Share It with Humility and Joy**
Whether you send it in a group chat, print it for team night, or read it aloud before rehearsal—share from a place of love, not pressure. You're not preaching; you're watering the hearts of fellow priests. Stay gentle. Stay authentic.

**7. Invite Others to Contribute**
You don't have to do it all! Encourage team members to write a week's devotional too. When everyone contributes, ownership grows. And sometimes, the most unexpected voices carry the most anointed words.

**Bonus Tips:**

- ✓ Keep it under 500 words—concise but rich.
- ✓ Use modern-day examples or fictional names to make it relatable.
- ✓ Be sure it always points back to Jesus.

**Final Encouragement:**

Writing devotionals isn't about perfection—it's about presence. It's about pausing as a team to say: *We are not just musicians. We are ministers. We're not just practicing notes. We're preparing hearts.*

So go ahead. Write. Share. Speak life. And let the fire on the altar never go out.

"The fire must be kept burning on the altar continuously; it must not go out." – Leviticus 6:13

Absolutely! Below is Appendix C: Worship Set Planning Template, designed to help worship leaders plan with intentionality, flow, and spiritual discernment. Following the template, I've also included a few sample setlists for different types of worship services and moments. Everything is presented in a practical, easy-to-use, and spiritually-aligned format.

---

# Appendix B: Worship Set Planning Template

**Purpose of this Template:**
This planning guide is not just about choosing songs. It's about stewarding a journey into the presence of God. A well-thought-out setlist is more than a musical lineup—it's a crafted experience where people are led to see Jesus more clearly, surrender more fully, and worship more freely.

---

**WORSHIP SET PLANNING FORM**

Date of Service: ______________________________

Theme / Sermon Topic (if any):

______________________________________________

Service Type: ☐ Sunday AM ☐ Sunday PM ☐ Youth ☐ Prayer ☐ Special Event

Pastoral/Preacher Input:

______________________________________________

Scripture Focus (if known):

______________________________________________

Worship Leader:

______________________________________________

Team Members (vocalists, band, tech):

_________________________________________

---

**1. Spiritual Direction**

- ✓ What is God highlighting this week? (e.g., surrender, joy, breakthrough, healing)
  *Write your personal sense or team's discernment here:*

- ✓ Is there a prophetic word or Scripture that informs the atmosphere?

*Example: Psalm 24 for a "King of Glory" emphasis*

---

## 2. Set Flow Strategy

- ✓ Opening Moment
  *A song that awakens the room and unites hearts with celebration or expectation.*
- ✓ Engagement / Build
  *Songs that invite participation and lift faith.*
- ✓ Heart of Worship / Intimacy
  *A slower-paced song or spontaneous moment focused on surrender or awe.*
- ✓ Ministry or Prayer Time Song (if applicable)
  *A responsive song to support the altar call or prophetic moment.*
- ✓ Closing Declaration / Sending
  *A faith-filled anthem or reprise to leave people strengthened.*

---

## 3. Setlist (Song Order)

| # | Song Title | Key | Flow Type | Transitions / Notes |
|---|---|---|---|---|
| 1 | | | | |
| 2 | | | | |
| 3 | | | | |
| 4 | | | | |
| 5 | | | | |

Flow Type Guide: Upbeat / Mid-tempo / Reflective / Spontaneous / Prophetic / Closing

Optional Additions:

- Scripture Reading Moment:
- Spoken Exhortation / Prayer Points:
- Spontaneous Worship Plan:
- Team Encouragement / Pre-brief Notes:

---

**4. Practical Logistics**

- ✓ Song Keys Aligned? Y / N
- ✓ Cues and Transitions Practiced? Y / N
- ✓ Lyrics and Chords Prepared? Y / N
- ✓ Slides, Media, and Visuals Ready? Y / N
- ✓ Instrument Changes / Pads / Clicks Prepped? Y / N
- ✓ Prayer Time Coordination (if needed)? Y / N

---

**5. Team Prayer Focus for the Week**

What will your team be interceding for before this service?

Encourage everyone to pray through the setlist—not just rehearse it.

# SAMPLE SETLISTS

**Sample 1: Sunday Morning Celebration**

**Theme**: Victory & God's Faithfulness

**Set Goal**: Stir faith, celebrate who God is, build unity in worship.

- ✓ *This Is Amazing Grace* – Key of Bb – (Opener, energetic)
- ✓ *Great Things* – Key of C – (Praise build)
- ✓ *Goodness of God* – Key of G – (Reflective, gratitude)
- ✓ *King of My Heart* – Key of C – (Ministry moment, personal declaration)
- ✓ *Firm Foundation (He Won't)* – Key of D – (Closing anthem)

---

**Sample 2: Revival Night / Extended Worship**
**Theme:** Holy Hunger & Encounter
**Set Goal:** Create space for God to move freely, extended moments of spontaneous worship.

- ✓ *Holy Spirit* – Key of D – (Welcome presence)
- ✓ *Worthy of It All* – Key of A – (Throne-room worship)
- ✓ *I Exalt Thee / Spontaneous* – Key of C – (Flow / open worship)
- ✓ *The More I Seek You* – Key of F – (Deep intimacy)
- ✓ *Spirit Break Out* – Key of Bb – (Prophetic declaration)
- ✓ *Fresh Wind* – Key of G – (Intercession for revival)

---

**Sample 3: Youth Service**
**Theme**: Identity in Christ
**Set Goal**: Energetic, fresh, gospel-centered with space to respond.

- ✓ *Glorious Day* – Key of A – (Testimony opener)
- ✓ *Who You Say I Am* – Key of E – (Identity in Christ)
- ✓ *Run to the Father* – Key of C – (Response altar moment)
- ✓ *Gratitude* – Key of G – (Simple closing)

---

**Sample 4: Communion / Reflective Service**
**Theme:** The Cross & Redemption
**Set Goal**: Lead hearts to reflect deeply on Jesus' sacrifice.

- ✓ *The Old Rugged Cross* – Key of G – (Traditional reverence)
- ✓ *Jesus Paid It All* – Key of C – (Reflective)

- ✓ *Thank You Jesus for the Blood* – Key of Bb – (Powerful cross-centered moment)
- ✓ *When I Survey the Wondrous Cross* – Key of D – (Communion support)

# Appendix C: Monthly Worship Review Checklist

**Purpose:**
This monthly review is not about perfection. It's about growth, alignment with God's presence, and unity within the team. Use it to celebrate wins, address areas for improvement, and seek the Spirit's guidance for future worship experiences.

---

## ☑ SECTION 1: SPIRITUAL CLIMATE

- ☐ Was there a sense of **God's presence** in the worship experience?
- ☐ Did the setlist reflect the **theme or message** of the service?
- ☐ Were there any **prophetic moments** or Spirit-led shifts during worship?
- ☐ Were worshippers engaged, participatory, and drawn toward Jesus?
- ☐ Was the team prepared spiritually through **prayer or devotion** before leading?
- ☐ Were moments of **spontaneous or heartfelt worship** handled with discernment

## ☑ SECTION 2: TEAM DYNAMICS & PREPARATION

- ☐ Was **rehearsal effective** and respectful of everyone's time?
- ☐ Did the team members come prepared with their **parts learned**?
- ☐ Did the team display **unity, humility, and grace** toward each other?
- ☐ Was there clear communication between **leader, vocalists, band, and tech**?
- ☐ Did everyone know the **flow of the service** in advance?

## ☑ SECTION 3: TECHNICAL QUALITY

- ☐ Were **sound levels balanced** and clear throughout the service?
- ☐ Were **transitions smooth** between songs and service elements?
- ☐ Were lyrics/screens/visuals correctly synced and visible?
- ☐ Did any **equipment malfunctions** occur? If so, were they handled calmly?
- ☐ Was there a clear **signal to start and stop** each song?

## ☑ SECTION 4: OVERALL EXPERIENCE

- ☐ What worked well this month?
- ☐ What needs improvement?
- ☐ Was feedback from the pastor or congregation received and discussed?
- ☐ What new songs were introduced or planned?
- ☐ What spiritual themes should we focus on next month?
- ☐ Are there any **training needs** or **team concerns** to address?

**Reflection Notes** (Optional space to capture God-moments, learning opportunities, or unusual occurrences.)

---

---

# Sample Monthly Worship Review 1 – June:
# Youth Revival Night

**Theme:** Awakening and Hunger for God
**Team Lead**: Sarah Paul
**Pastor's Message**: "Come Alive – Dry Bones Live" (Ezekiel 37)
**Setlist Highlights:**

- ✓ *Rattle!* – Key of B
- ✓ *Fresh Wind* – Key of C
- ✓ *Rest on Us* – Key of A
- ✓ *You Deserve It All (Spontaneous Flow)*

SPIRITUAL CLIMATE:

- ✓ The atmosphere was electrifying; the teens responded immediately by singing, clapping, and kneeling during *Fresh Wind*.
- ✓ During *You Deserve It All*, a few young people began praying for one another spontaneously—pastor later confirmed this was a Holy Spirit moment.

TEAM DYNAMICS:

- ✓ The team fasted and prayed together on Friday evening. Unity was high.
- ✓ Small miscommunication on song transitions, but handled well mid-set.

TECHNICAL OBSERVATIONS:

- ✓ Bass guitar cable came loose during the 2nd song—quickly replaced.
- ✓ Lyrics team was caught off-guard with spontaneous portion but recovered.

LEARNINGS:

- ✓ Schedule a mid-week sync for tech and music teams.
- ✓ Encourage back-up gear checks before worship.
- ✓ Incorporate short team prayer huddle backstage even on busy nights.

OVERALL SCORE: 9/10

Next Month Focus: Healing and Rest (Set planning around Isaiah 53)

---

## Sample Monthly Worship Review 2 – March: Sunday Morning Service

**Theme:** The Faithfulness of God
**Team Lead:** David Samuel
**Sermon Topic:** "God of the Generations"
**Setlist Highlights:**

- ✓ *This Is Amazing Grace* – Key of Bb
- ✓ *Faithful You Are* – Key of G
- ✓ *Great Is Thy Faithfulness* – Key of C
- ✓ *Promises* – Key of A

SPIRITUAL CLIMATE:

- ✓ Congregation entered worship quickly and seemed moved during *Great Is Thy Faithfulness*.
- ✓ Spontaneous Scripture reading by the worship leader reinforced the message beautifully.

TEAM DYNAMICS:

- ✓ Strong prep. Everyone arrived early and ready.
- ✓ New vocalist (Asha) was warmly welcomed and did well on harmonies.

TECHNICAL OBSERVATIONS:

- ✓ Sound check was smooth. Levels held steady throughout service.
- ✓ New lighting cues tested successfully.

LEARNINGS:

- ✓ Continue training for Scripture flow in between songs.
- ✓ Introduce new song *Promises* again next month to reinforce engagement.

OVERALL SCORE: 8.5/10

Next Month Focus: Introduce two new songs slowly—one upbeat, one reflective.

---

**Tips for Using This Checklist:**

Meet monthly as a team or at least with key leaders to reflect and refine.

Keep all reviews in a digital folder for annual assessment.

Use the review to celebrate God's faithfulness—don't just focus on problems.

Use findings to mentor new leaders, develop systems, and train others in excellence.

# Monthly Worship Review Scorecard (Appendix C - Scorecard Version)

**Purpose:**

This scorecard enables worship leaders and teams to track consistency, excellence, and spiritual sensitivity throughout the year. Use it alongside the checklist to measure specific elements from each worship service with prayerful reflection.

## 🔢 Scoring System:

| Score | Meaning |
|---|---|
| 1 | Needs major improvement |
| 2 | Below expectations |
| 3 | Acceptable, but room to grow |
| 4 | Good, consistent |
| 5 | Excellent, Spirit-led, fully engaged |

### 📅 Scorecard Table (Fill Monthly)

| Category | Jan | Feb | Mar | Apr | May | Jun | Jul | Aug | Sep | Oct | Nov |
|---|---|---|---|---|---|---|---|---|---|---|---|
| Spiritual Atmosphere | | | | | | | | | | | |
| Congregational Engagement | | | | | | | | | | | |
| Team Preparation | | | | | | | | | | | |
| Unity and Attitude | | | | | | | | | | | |
| Tech Execution (Sound/Visuals) | | | | | | | | | | | |
| Transitions & Flow | | | | | | | | | | | |
| Pastoral Alignment | | | | | | | | | | | |
| Feedback/ Follow-Up Applied | | | | | | | | | | | |
| Team Spiritual Growth | | | | | | | | | | | |
| Song Choice/ Spiritual Fit | | | | | | | | | | | |

📈 **Optional Scoring Tracker:**

Add all category scores per month and calculate an average to watch for overall improvement.

| Month | Total Score | Average (Divide by 10) | Key Wins / Focus for Next Month |
|---|---|---|---|
| Jan | | | |
| Feb | | | |
| Mar | | | |
| Apr | | | |
| May | | | |
| Jun | | | |
| Jul | | | |
| Aug | | | |
| Sep | | | |
| Oct | | | |
| Nov | | | |
| Dec | | | |

## Usage Tips:

- ✓ Have team leaders or department heads fill this out after each monthly review meeting.
- ✓ Use the notes section to highlight testimonies, prophetic words, or conflict resolutions.
- ✓ Evaluate overall growth trends each quarter.
- ✓ Incorporate into your annual worship vision meeting to plan training, new songs, and team building activities.

# Appendix D
# Exhortations at Every Stage of Worship Session

## 20 Exhortations to Begin a Worship Session (START / INTRO)

1. *"Welcome, beloved! Today, we come not just to sing songs, but to encounter the Living God. Let's fix our hearts on Him who is worthy of our everything."*
2. *"Before the first note is played, take a deep breath—let's lay aside the weight of the week and enter into God's presence with great expectation."*
3. *"This is not a concert. This is holy ground. We've gathered for one reason—to worship Jesus with all that we are."*
4. *"God is already here—waiting, longing for your heart. Let's respond by giving Him our full attention."*
5. *"Come hungry, come thirsty—He promises to fill. Let's lift up the name that is above every name: Jesus."*
6. *"Heaven is watching, and God is listening. Let's begin with reverence and anticipation."*
7. *"You are not an audience. You are a choir of redeemed voices joining heaven's eternal song."*
8. *"Let's not wait for a slow build-up—right now, where you are, begin to whisper your gratitude to the Lord."*

9. *"Worship is our response to His worth. Let's respond today with our voices, our hearts, and our whole lives."*
10. *"Let's raise our voices—not because everything is perfect—but because He is perfect, and He is worthy."*
11. *"You don't need to earn His presence. He's already here. Let's draw near to Him with confidence."*
12. *"This is your invitation to let go of distraction and step into deep communion with God."*
13. *"Every breath is a gift from God—let's return it in praise."*
14. *"Let's not spectate—let's participate. Our God is too glorious to be watched from the sidelines."*
15. *"You were made to worship. It's your design, your calling, your joy."*
16. *"Let's begin with honor. Let's begin with awe. Our God is holy!"*
17. *"Whatever you walked in with, bring it before Jesus. He's here to meet with you."*
18. *"This moment is sacred. Let's give our full selves in surrender and joy."*
19. *"Let's not wait to feel something. Let's lift up the name of Jesus by faith, and let feelings follow."*
20. *"Welcome to the throne room. The King is in. Let's lift up His name."*

---

**20 Exhortations on THANKSGIVING (Entering His Gates)**

1. *"The gate into His presence is thanksgiving—let's enter with hearts overflowing with gratitude."*
2. *"Before we ask for anything, let's thank Him for everything He's already done."*
3. *"Think of one thing God has done for you this week—and thank Him aloud. That's where worship begins."*
4. *"Gratitude changes the atmosphere. Let's thank Him until joy rises."*
5. *"Thanksgiving repositions our hearts. It reminds us that He is faithful, always."*
6. *"Let's not take grace for granted. Let's give thanks for the blood of Jesus today."*
7. *"We thank You, Lord—not only for the big miracles but also for breath, for mercy, for new beginnings."*
8. *"Gratitude keeps our hearts soft. Let's return to that posture now."*
9. *"Don't wait for the music. Begin with your words—thank Him aloud right now."*
10. *"Gratitude isn't based on how we feel—it's based on what we know. God is good, and His love endures forever."*
11. *"Has He healed you? Delivered you? Been near in the storm? Then let thanks rise up like a flood."*
12. *"The enemy can't stand a thankful believer. Let's confuse him by giving God thanks even in trial."*
13. *"Father, thank You for today—for waking us up with purpose and for loving us without fail."*

14. *“He’s been better to us than we deserve. Let’s tell Him how grateful we are.”*
15. *“Thanksgiving brings alignment. It reminds us who holds our past, present, and future.”*
16. *“When we give thanks, we’re opening the gates of heaven. Let’s swing them wide right now.”*
17. *“In the Old Testament, thanksgiving was always part of the sacrifice. Let’s offer that sacrifice joyfully today.”*
18. *“Even if nothing changed around you, He’s still worthy of thanks. Let’s bless His name.”*
19. *“Sometimes the most powerful worship begins with a whispered, ‘Thank You, Lord.’”*
20. *“Thanksgiving resets our hearts and postures us for encounter. Let’s begin there.”*

---

**20 Exhortations on PRAISE**

1. *"Praise is loud. Praise is expressive. Let everything that has breath—praise the Lord!"*
2. *"Praise breaks chains—ask Paul and Silas! Let's raise a sound that shakes the ground!"*
3. *"Our God reigns—and that's reason enough to shout and sing."*
4. *"Let's praise Him not just for what He's done—but for who He is. He's faithful, holy, mighty, and near."*
5. *"There is no one like our God. Let's declare it together—with our voices, with our hands, with our whole being."*
6. *"Praise is a weapon. Use it now to push back darkness and proclaim the victory of Jesus."*
7. *"David danced before the Lord with all his might—let's praise like that today!"*
8. *"Praise Him like you're already on the other side of the battle—because the victory belongs to Him."*
9. *"The Bible says God inhabits the praises of His people. Let's give Him something to inhabit."*
10. *"This is not hype. This is holy. This is praise."*
11. *"Let's not praise like God is small. Let's praise like He rules the galaxies!"*
12. *"Our praise is a declaration that Jesus is Lord over every situation."*
13. *"Even when we don't see it, God is working. That's why we praise in faith."*
14. *"Let's praise with joy. Joy is not an emotion—it's a response to the goodness of God."*
15. *"Every clap, every shout, every movement says, 'You are worthy, Lord!'"*

16. *"When we praise, we align earth with heaven—because heaven is never silent!"*
17. *"Let's build a throne of praise in this place for the King of Kings to sit upon."*
18. *"You're not too tired to praise—praise refreshes your soul."*
19. *"God doesn't need our praise—but we need to praise. It shifts our whole being."*
20. *"Lift up a song. Lift up a shout. Praise Him like He's worthy—because He is!"*

---

**20 Exhortations on WORSHIP (Going Deeper)**

1. *"Worship is not about volume—it's about surrender. Let's bow our hearts before the King."*
2. *"Right now, let's forget the room, forget the lights, and fix our eyes on Jesus alone."*
3. *"Let's move past the outer courts into the Holy of Holies—into that deep place where it's just you and Him."*
4. *"This is the moment we pour out our oil. The fragrance of your worship matters to God."*
5. *"No performance. No pressure. Just presence. Let's worship Him in spirit and truth."*
6. *"The King is here. What will you bring before Him?"*
7. *"This is not a time to sing about God—this is a time to sing to Him. Face to face."*
8. *"In worship, we stop asking and start adoring. Let's lift up adoration to our beautiful Savior."*
9. *"Worship is when our hearts say, 'Jesus, You are enough.' Let's tell Him that now."*
10. *"Mary broke the jar and poured it all on Jesus. What can you pour out today in worship?"*
11. *"Worship is the language of lovers. Let your heart speak now."*
12. *"Take a moment. Close your eyes. Whisper His name. Let every word be for Him."*
13. *"In worship, the soul kneels—even if the body stands. Let's kneel before the greatness of our God."*
14. *"This is sacred space—don't rush it. Let's linger in His presence."*
15. *"Sometimes the most powerful worship is the quietest moment. Don't be afraid of the stillness."*

16. *"Our God is holy. Let's tremble before Him—not in fear, but in awe."*
17. *"This is where transformation happens—in the gaze of Jesus."*
18. *"Lay your burdens at His feet. Worship isn't just praise—it's surrender."*
19. *"As the incense of worship rises, so does His nearness. Let's draw close."*
20. *"This is not about us. This is all about Him. Let's adore the Lamb who is worthy."*

## About the Author
## 'GERARD ASSEY'

Gerard Assey is a Graduate in Economics, a PGD in Management (HRD) and holds a Doctorate in Leadership. Gerard holds several International Qualifications in Sales, Debt Collection, Training & Teaching, and is a 'Fellow' of the prestigious 'Institute of Sales & Marketing Management'-UK, a Certified NLP Practitioner, a 'Certified Trainer', an 'Accredited Management Teacher-Behavioral Sciences', a 'Certified Competency Facilitator', a 'Certified Management Consultant'- (the International credentials of a professional management consultant, awarded in accordance with global standards of the ICMCI); and a Certification from the University of Michigan in 'Successful Negotiation: Essential Strategies and Skills'

He is also a Member of the 'National Association of Sales Professionals' backed with several years experience in varied industries, both in India and Overseas. He also holds an 'Etiquette Consultant' Certification from the USA (by Sue Fox, Author of Best Seller: 'Business Etiquette for Dummies'. She has trained some of the top celebrities' world over). He was also a recipient of a scholarship for extensive training in Japan on 'Corporate Management for India'.

Gerard Assey is 'Founder & Chief Corporate Trainer' of the Group: **'Citius, Altius, Fortius Unlimited'**- an organization that **celebrated 20 years of Glorious Service** in 2021, focusing on 3 Core Competencies:

**People. Performance. Profit**; in functional areas of Sales & Marketing, HR & Organizational Development, covering Recruitment, Training & Consultancy!

Having managed organizations with large Sales Forces in India & Overseas, his specialization cover extensive areas of Sales Training (All levels - Presentation, Negotiation, Key/ Strategic Accounts Management & Managerial Skills for all sectors), Bid Proposal/ Capture Planning/ Management Trainings, Retail Sales, Customer Service & Customer Retention Programs, Training for Prevention & Collection of Debt, Self & Personal Development Programs (Time Management, Teamwork & Team Building, Business Etiquette & Personal Grooming, Leadership & Managerial Skills, People Management Skills, Train-the-Trainer etc), including preparation of Custom-designed Business Manuals for Internal (HR, Induction, and Sales etc) & External use (Instruction, User Manuals).

Gerard has successfully conducted over 6450 Trainings & Workshops (as of May '25) all across India, Middle East, Africa, Europe & S.E. Asia. Besides public programs conducted regularly, both in India & Overseas, he has some of the top names as clients whom he services from Single Owners to large Public & Government undertakings, covering all sectors, for their in-house needs.

His website: www.CollectionSkills.com is the only one in this part of the world to be featured in the 'Collections & Credit Risk Magazine-USA' under 'Who's Who in Training' and ranks TOP, along with other websites listed below on most search engines.

**Gerard is author of 192 books already (May 2025),** all the books being available on all online platforms and outlets as E-books and Paperbacks

**A few of our business related books:**

1. Bite-sized Bits on Commonsense Management
2. Heart to Heart on Life's Principles'
3. How to become a Successful Manager
4. The Sales Professionals' Master Workbook of S.Y.S.T.E.M.S
5. The Professional Business Email Etiquette Handbook & Guide
6. The Professional Business Video-Conferencing Etiquette Handbook & Guide
7. Professional Presentation Skills
8. Exceptional Customer Service
9. Professional Tele-Marketing Skills
10. Professional Debt Collection Skills
11. The G.R.E.A.T. Sales & Service Workbook
12. Sales Training Advantage for Results (*The Ultimate Sales Training Manual to enable you stand out as a S.T.A.R.*)
13. CEO Daily Planner & Organizer
14. The Sales Professionals' Master Daily Planner
15. The Professional Debt Collector's Master Daily Planner
16. My Daily Planner & Organizer
17. MY EMERGENCY INFORMATION RECORD (Family Emergency & Peace of Mind Planner)
18. The Ultimate Therapist & Counselors Planner and Organizer
19. Building an Ethical Workplace
20. Managing Relationships at Work
21. Managing Business Meetings Effectively
22. Effective Delegation Skills
23. Goal Setting for Success
24. B2B Selling by Email
25. Professional Business Etiquette & Grooming
26. Dining Etiquette & Table Manners
27. Effective Networking Skills
28. Grooming, Etiquette & Manners for Teens, Young Adults & Future Leaders
29. Inter-Personal Skills
30. Get Ready, Get Hired!
31. Selling in a Recession
32. Effective Receivables Management in an Economic Downturn!
33. Real Estate & Property Sales Training
34. Credit Sales & Accounts Receivable Management

35. Selling Skills for Real Estate & Property Advisors
36. Take G.R.E.A.T. C.A.R.E!
37. Spa, Salon & Health Club Selling Skills
38. Selling Travel, Holiday & MICE Services
39. Selling Skills for Spa's, Salons & Health Clubs
40. Retailing in Salons & Spas
41. Selling Holiday, Vacation, Tours & Packages
42. The Power of Sales Referrals
43. Selling Luxury
44. Technical Selling Skills
45. Financial Advisors Sales Training
46. Dealing with Burnout at Work Monopolize Your Markets
47. Selling to Affluent Customers
48. Growing up with Grace
49. Financial Selling Skills
50. *The Effective Manager's Guide: Key Skills to Thrive*
51. From Aspiring to Inspiring: A Guide for New Managers on the Rise
52. The Power of Focus
53. Selling with Integrity: Sell Like Jesus The Perfect Role Model!
54. 31 Habits of Champions: Your 31-Day Journey to Greatness
55. Rejecting Grasshopper Talk: From Grasshopper to Giant-Killer-*Defeating Giants Daily!*
56. Navigate the AI-Powered Future of Bid & Proposals: Up-Skill to Stay Relevant with Alternative Career Paths & Opportunities
57. Hiring Sales Winners
58. Present with Impact
59. Success Unlocked: *Breaking Free from Habits that Hold You Back*
60. Complaints to Cheers, Feedback to Gold: Mastering Complaints Management
61. Thriving Together: *Cultivating Diversity, Equity, and Inclusion*
62. Coaching Skills for Sales Managers
63. Soaring to Success in Business & Leadership: Swifter, Higher, Stronger!
64. From Classroom to Podium: A Student's Guide to Powerful Public Speaking & Presentation Skills
65. Developing Self-Discipline
66. The CEO's 31-Day Power Plan: Unlocking Success through Essential Traits

67. Credibility Matters
68. A Winning Attitude
69. Bid & Proposal Management Using AI
70. Sales Forecasting: A Practical & Proven Guide to Strategic Sales Forecasting
71. Elevate & Energize: *50 Dynamic & Fun Activities for Peak Workplace Morale*
72. 'Sales SOS! Sales on Fire! *30 Days to Conquer Chaos & the Nightmares of Success!'*
73. Mastering Sales Managerial Skills: *Building High-Performing Teams & Driving Exceptional Results*
74. Eagle-Eyed Leadership: Unleashing the Power of 31 Lessons from Eagles
75. The Ultimate Employee Training Guide: *Training Today, Leading Tomorrow*
76. Being More Accountable at Work
77. Creating a Culture of Continuous Improvement
78. Effective Questioning & Listening Skills
79. The Power of Value Selling
80. The Growth Mindset
81. Mastering Professional Help Desk Skills
82. The Power to Lead with Empathy
83. Being Prepared: The Key to Unlocking Success
84. Youthful Spark-Youth Energizers, Activities and Games-Igniting the Fun in Youth
85. Ignite your Motivation for Success
86. Elevate Your Executive Presence: *Your Roadmap to Executive Excellence*
87. Smart Decisions: *Mastering Problem Solving with Strategic Solutions for Business Success*
88. Strategic Planning: *Developing and Implementing Strategic Plans to Achieve Long-Term Business Goals*
89. The Power of Stay Interviews
90. Developing G.R.I.T.
91. Adaptability
92. Diagnosis- *A Key Skill for Leadership*
93. The Burnout-Proof Salesperson: *The Master Guide to Preventing Stress & Burnout*- Strategies for Thriving in Sales
94. Learning from Failure: *Keys to Success*
95. Customer Success Management
96. Overcoming the Killers of Motivation
97. The C-Suite Code: *Mastering Skills for Executive Excellence'*

98. Dealing with Difficult Customers
99. Unlocking Your Potential: Mastering the Top 20 Life Skills for a Brighter Future
100. Nurturing Tomorrow's Leaders: *Essential Soft Skills Every Child Must Learn*
101. Lively & Fun Party Games for Seniors & Elders
102. Role Playing for Sales Champions: From Practice to Performance
103. Fun and Exciting Party Games for Kids
104. Case Studies for Sales
105. Role-Playing for Unbeatable Customer Service
106. Case Studies in Customer Service
107. Case Studies in Winning Negotiations
108. Case Studies in Management & Leadership
109. Case Studies in Human Resources & Talent Management
110. CEO Success Blueprint: The Essential Toolkit for CEOs and C-Level Executives
111. The Salesperson's Self-Coaching Guide: *Master Your Own Self-Coaching Plan for Success*
112. Overcoming Procrastination: *Your Ultimate Guide to Stop Delaying and Start Living Your Best Life*
113. When True Colors Are Exposed: *The Journey to Unmasking Humanity*
114. Life-Changing Habits for Teens: Teen Success Blueprint for a Bright Future
115. Workplace Stress-Free: *Proven Strategies to Thrive at Work and Beyond*
116. Objection Overruled: *The Ultimate Guide to Turning 'No' into 'Yes'*
117. Building Strong Teams: *A Comprehensive Guide to Team Building*
118. Ethical & Moral Leadership in Business: *Eliminating Unethical Practices & Building a Culture of Trust & Integrity*

From the Ministry side, Gerard graduated in the very first batch of Charis Bible College-India & had for over 9 years served as a Part-time Faculty at Charis Bible College-Chennai (Andrew Wommack Ministries-Colorado, USA).
He also holds a Diploma in Worship (a subject closest to his heart) from the JSOW and is also a graduate of the Advanced Mentorship Program (AMP) and the Circle Of

Ministerial Engagement (C.O.M.E.) of Prophet Jerome Fernando and a Spiritual Son of the Esteemed Prophet. An accomplished author of several Secular & Christian Books, Gerard has been on the board of a few international organizations and boasts of being the SON of the MOST HIGH GOD: An ordinary guy following an extraordinary GOD!

**...And some of his most recent Christian Books being:**

1. A Bouquet of Praises for My KING
2. Christian Jokes for the Serious Religious' Folks!
3. Jesus Healed You!
4. Praise24Ever! (also in Tamil version)
5. The 5G Network of GOD
6. Building Faith over F.E.A.R- FACE EVERYTHING AND RISE with JESUS
7. Hebrew and Greek Praise and Worship Words
8. Godly Mothers' and Grandmothers' Bible Story time for Kids!
9. Miracles of Jesus in Pictures
10. Raise your Praise all 365 Days
11. Thanking GOD with an Attitude of Gratitude
12. Meditating on the Attributes of GOD
13. Puppet Scripts
14. Alcohol Ruins, JESUS Reforms, Renews & Restores!
15. Habakkuk 2:2 Christian Daily Journal, Planner & Organizer
16. ABC of GOD's Word for Handwriting Practice
17. Daily Bible Verse Handwriting Practice (Building Godly Character & Faith through Cursive Handwriting Practice!)
18. Guiding Light: Fun & Faith-Building Bible Activities for Children
19. Rejecting Grasshopper Talk: From Grasshopper to Giant-Killer-*Defeating Giants Daily!*
20. Teen Titans of Faith: *Building Courage, Determination & Christ-like-Esteem*
21. I AM Empowered: *Unleashing Divine Power with Positive Declarations*
22. Be A Solution Provider-*From Passion to Purpose*: *A Biblical Guide to Being the Answer to the World!*
23. Miracles of JESUS
24. Parables of Jesus for a Meaningful Life!
25. A Grateful Heart: Importance of Sharing Testimonies of GOD's Grace
26. Melodies of Worship to JESUS: 31 Songs of Praise & Worship From My Heart to HIS!
27. I AM SO BLESSED!
28. My Daily Cup of Energizer

29. 31 Leadership Lessons *from* Jesus- *The Supreme Leader*
30. Peace Amidst Storms: A Biblical Guide to Conquering S.T.R.E.S.S.
31. Rise Above: 20 Biblical Eagle Lessons for Life's Triumphs
32. Godly Goal Setting: *The FAITHFUL Blueprint for a Purpose-Driven Life*
33. The Profound Attributes of our Mighty GOD: Understanding the 10S's of the Almighty
34. Worship Now, Worship Forever: *A Journey from Earthly Praise to Eternal Glory*
35. Unceasing Praise & Worship: *365 Days to Worship the King*
36. The ROAR Within: *Living with Purpose and Authority through the Power of the Holy Spirit*
37. From Potential to Purpose: Unlocking and Multiplying Your Talents & Gifts for Kingdom Impact
38. Songs from the Heart: *Worshipping GOD in Your Own Tune & Melody*
39. Awakening Praise & Worship: Hebrew & Greek Words to Raise Your Praise
40. Sing a NEW Song to the LORD Everyday: *Daily Devotions of Praise & Worship to Lift Your Heart & Glorify HIS Name*
41. *The* A.R.O.M.A. of True Worship: *Creating Worship That Delights God*
42. Becoming A Kingdom Champion: *Embracing God's Call for a Life of Purpose & Victory*
43. The Busy Businessman's Daily Devotional: 366 Crisp Truths to Start Your Day Strong
44. The Teacher's Heart: *Daily Devotions for Educators*
45. Anchored! *A 31-Day Devotional for Students Facing Life's Challenges*
46. Suddenly! Unlocking Unorthodox Breakthroughs through Unusual Worship
47. Overcoming Adversity: *Lessons from the Bible for Modern Challenges*
48. LORD, Don't do it without me
49. Kingdom Leadership: *Biblical Principles for Modern Leaders*
50. Heartprints of God- *Growing God's Way:* Daily Devotions for Kids to Shine Bright
51. Send Judah First: Let your Praises Go up First to See the Mighty Move of GOD
52. DIVINE MOMENTS: *Recognizing, Embracing, Preparing, and Walking into Life-Changing Encounters with God*
53. Be a Builder in the Kingdom: *The C.E.M.E.N.T. Guide*

to Creating a Lasting Legacy

54. Unshakable: *Pillars of Godly Womanhood* (Pillars of Faith That Changed History)
55. Lead Like a Shepherd: *14 Essential Traits for Pastoral Excellence*
56. The Worship Leader's Arsenal: *Powerful Exhortations to Ignite Thanksgiving, Praise & Worship*
57. Women of UnShakable Faith: *31-Day Devotional for Strength, Purpose & Influence*
58. Called to Teach: *A Complete 10-Week Training Guide for Impactful VBS Teachers*
59. Strumming for the KING: Cowboy Songs of Faith & Fire
60. The Ultimate Youth Camp Playbook: *50 Bible-Centered Indoor Games to Engage, Equip, and Empower Teens*
61. Glad in HIS Presence: *David's Revelation of GOD's Love & Mercy*
62. The Spirit Behind the Sound: *52 Devotionals for Worship Teams*
63. THE COWBOY'S COMPASS: *Riding the Trail of Faith with Grit & Grace*
64. Worship as My Weapon: *Living Victoriously through the Power of Praise*
65. A Worshipper Always Wins: *Living a Life of Victorious Worship*
66. Worship That Leads to the Throne: *Practical Strategies for Worship Leaders to Inspire Their Team & Usher People into God's Presence*

Besides regularly contributing to business & trade journals, including international ones such as the 'Creative Training Techniques' and the 'Sales News' of the U.S.A, He is also a member of several prestigious bodies & trade associations, having participated in many Conferences & Workshops in India & Overseas.

Prior to his last assignment of leading & managing a large MNC as head, Gerard had a 3-year stint in the Middle East as a Consultant with a leading British Consultancy Firm.

As the past 'Official Country Representative' for the International Business Award- 'THE STEVIES'-(the business world's own Oscar) for about 4 years- he ensured a few Indian companies that qualify for the same every year!

Gerard can be contacted at:

Email: training@Sales-Training.in,training@CollectionSkills.com
Websites:

www.Sales-Training.in
www.EtiquetteWorks.in
www.CollectionSkills.com
www.RetailSalesTraining.in
www.SalesTrainingIndia.com
www.ManualPreparation.com
www.TrainingWithPuppets.com
www.FirstContactAcademy.com
www.SalesAndMarketingRecruiter.com

www.ingramcontent.com/pod-product-compliance
Ingram Content Group UK Ltd.
Pitfield, Milton Keynes, MK11 3LW, UK
UKHW020050200726
13845UKWH00055B/631

9 788198 697493